An Elephant
in the
Living Room

A Leader's Guide for Helping Children of Alcoholics

Marion H. Typpo, Ph.D.
Jill M. Hastings, Ph.D.

2415 Annapolis Lane, Minneapolis, Minnesota 55441

Library of Congress Catalog Card Number 84-70189
ISBN 0-89638-071-8

Cover design by Kristen McDougall

Inquiries, orders, and catalog requests should be addressed to
CompCare Publishers
2415 Annapolis Lane
Minneapolis, Minnesota 55441
Call 559-4800 or toll free 800/328-3330

7   8   9

91   92   93   94

Acknowledgments

The staff of the adult chemical dependency unit at St. Mary's Rehabilitation Center, Minneapolis, Minnesota, especially Dr. George Mann, Maureen Dudley Piekarski, Rachel Easton, Marion Mann, Rick Beresford, Pam Fogel, David Hiers, Bonnie Mulligan, Cal Scheidegger, Fr. George Coyan, and Sr. Helen Griffith.

The staff of the Family Counseling Center, Columbia, Missouri, especially Dr. John Small, Karen Yopp, Karen Schiess, Mary DuBose, and Fred Watts.

Also Don and Nancy Howard; Dr. Kristi Roberts; Sharon Bottorff; Gilbert and Amanda Lenz; Matthew and Lisa Boyer; Caryn and Melissa Mummert; John, Lisa, and Eric Typpo; the Hastings family; Scott Poethig; Arden and Rod Stephens; Cheryl Fried Meisterman, and Elizabeth Vemer.

A special thank you to our editor, Jane Thomas Noland, whose enthusiasm kept us going.

Names and identifying details have been changed to protect the anonymity of the children whose stories are told in this book.

Alcoholism:
An Elephant in the Living Room

Imagine an ordinary living room—chairs, couch, coffee table, a TV set, and, in the middle, a

LARGE, GRAY ELEPHANT

The ELEPHANT stands there, shifting from one foot to another and slowly swaying from side to side. Imagine also the people who live in this house: a child, along with a mother and/or father and maybe some sisters and brothers. All members of the family have to go through the living room many times each day and the child watches as they walk through the room very...carefully ...around...the...ELEPHANT. Everyone avoids the swinging trunk and enormous feet.

Since no one ever talks about the ELEPHANT, the child knows that she's not supposed to talk about it either. And she doesn't. Not to anyone.

But the child wonders why nobody is saying anything or doing anything to move the ELE-

PHANT. After all, it's a very big ELEPHANT and having to keep walking around it all the time is not easy. The child may even wonder if other people really see the ELEPHANT or if perhaps she made it up. But since she can't ask anyone about the ELEPHANT, she just keeps on wondering, walking around it, and worrying. She wishes she could talk to somebody about the ELEPHANT.

Living with alcoholism is a lot like living with an ELEPHANT IN THE LIVING ROOM. The accompanying *An Elephant in the Living Room,* The Children's Book provides a way for children to begin talking about the difficulties of living in a family where drinking or other drug abuse is a problem.

The effects of an alcoholic parent on a child's development can be devastating. Children from alcoholic families need emotional support, intervention, and treatment. Yet historically counseling has focused on the adult alcoholics and their problems. Only about five percent of the children of alcoholics receive any kind of treatment or program of support (Korcok, 1981).

The two companion books which share the title, *An Elephant in the Living Room,* include a workbook for elementary-aged children and this guide for leaders of children's groups. The books and the program they comprise were designed to help adult professionals and paraprofessionals help children of alcoholics. Specifically, the materials were developed to meet needs expressed by:

• counselors and group leaders in an alcohol/drug dependency treatment setting or counseling center who are well versed in the disease and treatment of alcoholism but are less familiar with child development and family relations;

• counselors, teachers, or social workers—especially in a school setting—who understand children and their development but have less familiarity with alcoholism/chemical dependency and its effects on the family.

These two perspectives are interdependent and essential if one is to work with children who are trying to understand, cope with, and grow up in the confusion of a family which has an ELEPHANT in the living room—an ELEPHANT called alcoholism.

Contents

Chapter One: Children at Risk 1
  FAS children and abuse 4
  The symptom of silence 4
  The disease concept 5
  A family disease 6
  Purposes of these books 7

Chapter Two: Family Myths and Models 11
  Functional families 23
  Dysfunctional families 24
  Authority and power 27
  Parenting and family roles 29
  Children and family stress 32

Chapter Three: Children and Change 35
  Physical growth and maturation 39
  Fetal Alcohol Syndrome 41
  Cognitive changes 42
  Social skills 54
    Roles within the families 54
    Friendships 60

Chapter Four: Helping Children of Alcoholics   67
  In alcoholism treatment centers 68
  In general children's support groups 70

In school settings 72
An important caution 76
Suggestions for setting up groups 77
  Physical setting 77
  Ages of children 78
  Size of group 78
  Number and length of sessions 79
  Group leaders 79
Explaining groups to parents 83
Using The Children's Book with an
individual child 90
Reporting child abuse and neglect 91
Working with handicapped children 94

Chapter Five: Using The Children's Book ... 103
  Initial session 104
  Confidentiality 106
  Chapter 1: Drinking and Drugs 107
  Chapter 2: Feelings 109
  Chapter 3: Families 111
  Chapter 4: Coping with Problems 116
  Chapter 5: Changes 117
  Chapter 6: Choices 118
  Evaluation 119
  The end or the beginning? 120
  About the authors 121

References 123
Additional Resources 126
  Books and bibliographies 126
  Other publications 127
  Films 127
  Model programs 128
  Organizations 128

Chapter One
Children at Risk

Shauna, a thirteen-year-old daughter of an alcoholic, wrote:

"My family has this problem we can't seem to solve, and it's making everybody kind of crazy."

Peter, age eleven, whose mother has a drinking problem, wrote:

"It makes you feel neglected, left out. You feel out of place in the family. Sometimes it makes you feel mad, sad, frustrated, helpless and useless, hurt, sick. It makes you feel like you're in the middle of a war."

Shauna and Peter are two of approximately 15 million American children under age twenty who have an alcoholic parent. This would mean that four to six out of any classroom of twenty-five children live in alcoholic homes, homes which house at least one alcoholic or drug-dependent family member (Korcok, 1981). And the number seems to be increasing.

The households of alcoholic families, with their unpredictability and confusion, are difficult places for children to live in and grow. Birthday cakes may not get baked. The Tooth Fairy may not remember the dime or quarter. Even Santa Claus's visits may be stressful and unhappy. The interior of an alcoholic family provides a distorted view of "normal" family life for the children who live there.

Researchers point out that the future for children living in alcoholic families—unless they are given some kind of treatment or support—does not look bright. Children of alcoholics are shown to be at high risk for a) marrying alcoholics, or b) becoming alcoholic themselves.

It is very difficult to combine statistics meaningfully to determine just how many such children there are. One estimate suggests that fifty percent of all alcoholics have or have had at least one alcoholic parent (Korcok, 1981). Suffice it to say that children in alcoholic families are particularly vulnerable to alcoholism and the likelihood of their being included in the next generation of alcoholics is great. These children surely constitute an appropriate target group for prevention efforts. Just how many of these children there are is hard to know.

These children of alcoholics also risk developing serious psychosocial problems. Miller and Jang (1977) in their study of children from poor, urban, multi-problem families found that children from alcoholic families had greater socialization difficulties than did children from nonalcoholic families, even though all were from the same multi-problem group. The children were more likely to have run away from home, been suspended or expelled from school, and had shown more frequent signs of emotional strain. Interestingly, not one child in this study had ever participated in Al-Anon or Alateen activities, although most knew about them.

As adults, these children still were doing less well. They were more likely to have failed in marriage, in their work, and in their ability to support themselves and their families. While more sons than daughters tended to become heavy drinkers, in families in which only the mother was alcoholic more daughters than sons drank heavily. The parenting role of the mother appeared to be crucial in determining the drinking patterns of her daughter. When both parents were alcoholic, over half the sons and one third of the daughters became heavy drinkers.

Children aged nine to twelve in alcoholic families registered lower in self-concept and self-esteem than did peers with nonalcoholic parents (Baraga, 1977). In a study of adolescents with alcoholic parents (Hughes, 1977), results indicated that children of alcoholic parents often suffered from negative emotional moods, low self-esteem, and poor social judgment.

The majority of alcoholic parents seem to have difficulty in child-rearing. Alcohol does play a significant role in child abuse and neglect (Woodside, 1982). Alcohol is often linked to child homicide.

The influence of alcohol can be seen in the physical abuse of children or spouse, in the inconsistent and erratic parenting that is a part of child neglect, both physical and emotional, and in child sexual abuse and incest. Of course, not all alcoholic parents abuse or neglect their children, but these are very real concerns.

FAS children and abuse

A link also has been suggested between child abuse and the Fetal Alcohol Syndrome (FAS) or Fetal Alcohol Effects (FAE). FAS is a group of symptoms (including mental retardation, small head, skinny arms and legs, peculiar facial characteristics, and other physical abnormalities) which may show up in children whose mothers drank during pregnancy. A child who does not have the full range of symptoms (FAS) still may show some of these defects (FAE). Developmental handicaps may make an FAS child a vulnerable and likely target for abuse.

The symptom of silence

One of the symptoms of alcoholism in families is silence—children of alcoholics have learned not to talk about their problems, not with other family members, not with friends, not with teachers or others who might help. They just feel bad all by themselves!

However, according to both the Baraga and Hughes studies mentioned earlier, one encouraging note for children who attend Alateen was that membership in that internationally recognized program of support for children from alcoholic families was predictive of a higher self-concept. Providing emotional support and a place to talk things out did seem to improve these children's feelings about themselves.

The disease concept

For years this conspiracy of silence went hand in hand with traditional attitudes about alcoholism. Alcoholism had been seen as a moral problem, a weakness or lack of will power. Only in the past half century has alcoholism been termed a disease. This acceptance of alcoholism as a disease has been helpful because an etiology, symptoms, typical course, and a predictable prognosis have been identified. The disease concept transformed alcoholism from a moral problem into a medical problem, which made way for the development of treatment for alcoholic and other drug-dependent individuals.

A family disease

While the focus of alcoholism treatment was—and still is in some places—the alcoholic individual, more recently alcoholism/chemical dependency has been recognized as a condition which affects the entire family. *An Elephant in the Living Room* is based on the concept that alcoholism is indeed a family disease and that *all* family members—including children—need assistance in their recovery.

These non-drinking family members are often called co-alcoholic or co-dependent. The family is an interdependent and interconnected system in which all members, young and old, are integral and active parts. Each member's actions influence other individual members and the working of the system as a whole. Children are not only influenced by adult family members, but they actively influence the behavior of the adults.

Some family systems are functional—they seem to work well. Others are dysfunctional. An alcoholic family usually does not work well as a system. Nor does it do an adequate job in caring for the needs of its members. Alcoholism, as it produces a massive denial of the drinking, pulls the family system out of balance and symmetry.

Because alcoholism/chemical dependency is a family disease, recovery is a family process. In treatment, children, as well as adults, can be taught more effective coping behaviors and interpersonal skills. Young members from an alcoholic family can learn ways to handle the worrisome and painful situations they often face at home, as well as their feelings about them.

When children cannot rely on their own family system to give them the nurturing, respect, and love they need, they can be guided to seek support in the wider community in which they live.

Purposes of these books

These two books, the adult book for group leaders and the companion children's book, share the title: *An Elephant in the Living Room.* They have been designed to help children from about seven years old to early adolescence who live in families in which there is an alcoholic mother or father or sibling. The Children's Book, intended for use only in conjunction with the background material provided in the adult book, can be used for working with children in a group or as an aid for counseling an individual child. The adult book is A Leader's Guide for counselors, teachers, or other helping adults who facilitate children's support groups or work individually with children of alcoholics.

These materials were developed in cooperation with the counselors and clients of the St. Mary's Rehabilitation Center's adult chemical dependency unit in Minneapolis, Minnesota, and the Family

Counseling Center in Columbia, Missouri. St. Mary's Hospital has both inpatient and outpatient programs for alcoholic and other drug-dependent persons and their families. The Family Counseling Center is an outpatient center for alcoholics and their families.

Children, too, had a hand in designing these materials. The first draft of The Children's Book was tested with thirty-six children between the ages of five and twelve. Although the program was designed for children of approximately seven to twelve years of age, younger children initially were included in the group sessions to help determine an appropriate lower age limit for the materials. In this first sample group, thirteen children had alcoholic mothers, twenty had alcoholic fathers, one had both an alcoholic mother and an alcoholic father, and two had alcoholic siblings.

Also, meetings were arranged with a total of fifty-seven teenagers, who were divided into small groups to discuss the problems of living with alcoholic parents. Since these adolescents were better able than the younger children to verbalize their past and present feelings, they contributed greatly to the development of the materials.

The books which evolved—out of the expertise and concern of professionals and the experiences of children themselves—aim specifically to help children:

- understand that alcoholism is a disease, and that they are not the cause of this disease;

- realize that they are not alone, that other children are coping with similar problems;

- learn to recognize their feelings and express them appropriately;

- improve their self-esteem by recognizing their strengths and abilities;

- improve their relationships with parents and siblings;

- develop some practical ways of coping with typical problems in alcoholic families;

- improve their ability to make good decisions and to exercise what control they can in their lives, in order to reduce their feelings of powerlessness.

The group counseling approach tries, first of all, to overcome the heartbreaking sense of isolation which many of these children feel—isolation which may deprive them of the ability to enjoy trusting, loving relationships in years ahead. The inability to achieve or maintain intimacy in relationships is a recurring complaint of adult children of alcoholics.

Chapter Two
Family Myths and Models

Almost everybody "knows" about families since most of us grew up in them. The beliefs we hold about what families are like and what they do are linked to our personal histories and also to our expectations about what families-in-general are like. However, some of our beliefs about families-in-general are myths, more grounded in assumptions or wishes than in reality. Since alcoholic families are *families* first of all, it would seem important to identify some of these family myths so that our vision may be clearer and our expectations based in reality.

Family Myth Number One:
Normal families can easily be distinguished from abnormal ones.

The term "normal" can have a rainbow-range of meanings. Sometimes "normal" describes "what everybody else does." "Normal" families talk over their problems, never get mad at their children, keep their basements neat, and always pay bills on time—or so we think. Because we can't always see behind the walls to view the inner workings of a household and the family who lives there, most of us assume others are managing better and getting along more smoothly than we are. We compare our own real family lives to the mythical family lives of others, since we see and hear only those behaviors and feelings that people allow us to see or hear.

What we see is "onstage" rather than "offstage" behavior (Goffman, 1959). We display "onstage" behavior for a job interview or parent-teacher conference, for a gathering of invited friends when we present a clutter-free family room and polite conversation. We lapse into "offstage" behavior when our visitors leave, as we sigh, kick off our shoes, and re-spread newspapers back on the floor where they were before the company appeared.

Since we usually see others "onstage," our mythical view is that other people's private lives are the same as their public lives—that our neighbors always behave the way they do when we're with them. If we really believe this, then comparing ourselves to them inevitably will be negative.

Because "onstage" and "offstage" behaviors in alcoholic families are often confused and overlapping, these families suffer even more through such comparisons. Two kinds of assumptions about alcoholic families are often made. We may assume that any appalling alcoholic behavior seen in public—inebriated lurchings, noisy threats, inappropriate tears—goes on all of the time at home. The other assumption—much more inhibiting for family members seeking help—is that the family's "normal" public behavior is a valid indication that there are no problems at home.

For instance, Janice, the seventh-grade daughter of an alcoholic father, in desperation told her junior high school counselor that she thought her dad had a drinking problem and asked for advice. The counselor responded incredulously, "Oh, that can't be true. I know your father and he is such a nice man!" Besides reinforcing another myth, that alcoholics are not "nice" persons, this gave Janice two problems to contend with—her father's alcoholism and her counselor's denial that a problem existed!

Family Myth Number Two:
Differences within families are settled
by consensus, not by conflict.

Families are places where growth and development take place. Children are not the only ones who change. Adults get older too and change roles or jobs or responsibilities. Timetables for growth and agendas for change create differences of opinion and generate conflicting pulls and pushes. Indeed, change and conflict are characteristics of human development and are facets of all social systems, including the family.

Therefore, differences of opinion or conflicting ideas are not necessarily bad. Only when conflict is not discussed or settled, when it escalates to open warfare or hides behind unfair and sneaky guerrilla tactics does it become damaging. Rather than being suppressed or contained, conflict needs to be aired, discussed, and understood.

In alcoholic families, however, conflict often has come to dominate the family or to manifest itself destructively or subversively. Differences are seldom talked about. Children may never have heard adults disagree honestly, debate or argue, and then resolve an issue. Wilson and Orford (1978) found that children of alcoholics reported that the fighting and quarreling in the house were major concerns—even greater concerns than the drinking itself.

Greg, age eleven, said, "I wouldn't have minded the fighting so much if it had solved anything or made things better. But it didn't. It just went on...and on...and on."

The point at which family conflict becomes truly destructive for a child varies and may be related to age, sex, or other factors. Some children just have a lower threshold of toleration for discord. We should remember too that each child lives in a psychologically somewhat different family. As Jessie Bernard (1975) pointed out, every marriage is really composed of two marriages—his and hers—and that the two are not the same. In a similar way, one child's family may be entirely different from a sibling's family, even though the two live in presumably "the same" family situation.

Family Myth Number Three: Communication within a family is natural and easy.

Each family has its own unique set of words, definitions, and rules by which its members communicate. Good communication requires honesty and trust, qualities that often are in short supply in dysfunctional families.

A common communication breakdown in alcoholic families comes from the family members' denial of the drinking problem (overlooking the ELEPHANT). Family members know the family secrets, all right, but never discuss them.

Roger, thirteen, reported coming home with his mother and younger brother to find his father passed out in the living room with furniture in disarray and dishes scattered all around him. No one said a word while the mess was quietly cleaned up and his mother went to get a blanket to put over his father. Nothing was said the following morning either.

This kind of denial serves a purpose. It is one way of dealing with pain without having to face reality. Roger's mother did not want to face the possibility of her husband's alcoholism. If she admitted the possibility, then she would have to talk to her sons about it.

Children find this denial of what's real extremely troubling. Have they only imagined what they saw? Is it not important? Why the silence?

Children also are confused when two opposing messages are given. In this kind of double-bind communication, usually one message is verbal, the other behavioral. A parent may say, "Just do what you like. Don't worry about me," but the behavior—a martyred, long-suffering sigh—seems to negate the words. "Be spontaneous," might be the verbal message from a parent whose barrenly neat household and rigid reactions to new ideas seem to preclude spontaneity. In no-win situations like these, a child obviously cannot carry out both the verbal and the behavioral messages. Double-message-giving may be especially common in alcoholic families, where the victims of alcoholism, as well as the nonalcoholic adults affected by it, are out of touch with their real feelings.

Dysfunctional communication also can mean simply not listening, not hearing what another person is saying. Preoccupied or weary adults find it easy to ignore children this way. Or an adult may mislabel a situation or an emotion for a child, perhaps proclaiming that a child is hungry or sleepy or angry when the child is not. Such ignoring or mislabeling tells a child clearly that his feelings—for that matter, he himself—is not worthy of much notice.

Another way that a parent can be verbally confusing to a child is to ask for something that is really in the parent's own interest but insist that it is for the child's sake. A mother may tell a child, "It's time you went to bed, dear, because you've had a hard day," when, in fact, the child has had a very ordinary, non-taxing day and the parent merely wants the child out of the way.

Children do try to make sense out of the world they live in. Often they will have these mixed messages figured out. But *how* they figure them out, the meaning they attach to them, will depend on many factors, including their own ages and personalities and the specific situations. A child's self-esteem can suffer from such poor or baffling communication.

Children from alcoholic families may never have been involved in good communication. The possibility of being open and honest in verbal interactions with others may come as a revelation to them. For these children, being open and honest will take practice and time. A group program like this one can be a place to begin.

Family Myth Number Four: There is — and
there has always been — a "right kind" of
family. And a corollary: Families today
have departed from the norm; they are
breaking apart and disintegrating,
compared with the "strong" families of the
past.

Many people are wringing their hands over the
demise of the family. However there always have
been families in which both parents were absent
during the day or worked outside the home; families made smaller by death, divorce, or separation;
families with fathers who were away for long
periods of time.

We are concerned about the current divorce
rate, but if we look back to the turn of the century we find that marital disruption due to the
death of a spouse was about as common then as
disruption due to divorce is today (Bane, 1976).

Years ago families usually had nonfamily members living with them — boarders, hired help, shirt-
tail relatives. Most of these living arrangements
came about simply because of necessity. Elderly
people lived with younger ones often because they
had no other options.

Fixed ideas about the "right" kind of family,
about who ought to be included in the household
and how relationships should function, probably

are more of a hindrance than a help to constructive change.

Perhaps, after all, there never *was* a "golden age of the family."

The family changes and flexes in response to outside pressures as well as to expectations held by people within it. The roles family members assume and the way they carry out family life depend on differences in structure and expectations. It would be simplistic to say that alcoholism is the result of a broken home. People are faced with events or situations, try to understand them, then act on whatever interpretations they fashion. If an adult believes that she drinks or takes pills because "my mother loved me but she died" or "we lived on the wrong side of the tracks and I never had a chance" or some similar rationale, however erroneous, *that is* the justification and explanation *for her.*

Therefore it is important to intervene with a child before beliefs like these have had time to solidify into convictions. Children in alcoholic families need to be helped to realize that what is one person's reality or "reason" does not have to be another's.

As there may well be no "typical" or "right" kind of family, there may well be no "typical" alcoholic family. The children in the group share one major characteristic: they are all trying to live in alcoholic families. But their families may be different in makeup, expectations, and roles.

Family Myth Number Five:
There are "good" parents and "bad"
parents, in the same predetermined
way that some of us have blue eyes
and others brown.

In truth, a parenting situation is far more complex. A parent-child relationship is exactly that—a relationship determined by the child as well as the adult. Differences in children trigger or elicit different parenting behaviors. A shy, quiet, withdrawn child probably will be parented differently than will a bouncy, boisterous one. Thus:

Given this perspective, we are not surprised to see very different kinds of child behaviors, as well as parent behaviors, within one family.

We're accustomed to hearing about parenting styles—permissive, democratic, or authoritarian—as though style were the only dimension of parenting. But more important than style is congruence. "Good" parenting happens when there is a congruence, a "fit" between parent and child. The parent is sensitive to situations as they appear to the child, and the child is receptive to the concerns of the parent.

In an alcoholic family, some of this sensitivity on a parent's part may be lessened, perhaps dulled by the alcohol or other drug use. The nondrinking or co-alcoholic parent's sensitivity to the child's needs may be pushed aside by the overwhelming problems of living with an alcoholic. Parents may not discriminate between the kinds of parenting needed by different children. As adults in an alcoholic family struggle with their own problems, parenting may become less sensitive, more authoritarian and power-based. Finally, there may be greater style "swings," from permissive and flexible one day to autocratic and unapproachable the next. Obviously this is hard for children to understand.

As a group leader, you may hear about some of these parental behaviors from the children you are working with. In spite of such inconsistencies, whenever possible you can reinforce positively—for children and parents too—the mother's or father's willingness to allow a child's participation in the group as an indication of responsible parenting.

As all members of alcoholic families, young and old, accept the concept of alcoholism as a disease that affects the entire family, they can work past this myth of "good" and "bad" parenting and get on with the task of family recovery.

Family Myth Number Six:
What goes on in other people's
families is no one's business but theirs.

This belief in family privacy is responsible for our turning our backs not only on alcoholism, but on a multitude of alcohol-related instances of wife-battering and abuse and neglect of children and the elderly. Breaking through this myth to a shared, societal awareness of responsibility for intervention and treatment is all-important if we are to offer choices to children of alcoholics. Teachers, counselors, pastors, health professionals, law officers, neighbors—all who are concerned—have an obligation to put aside this myth of family privacy and do what they can to offer understanding and the possibility of change to children living in alcoholic homes. The opportunities to make choices may not be available within an alcoholic family. If this is so, they must come from outside—from other people who care.

Family models

We have seen that "normal" vs. "abnormal" or "good" vs. "bad" are not very useful ways to differentiate between families. A better perspective might be to consider functional families and dysfunctional ones.

Functional families

Functional families are able to meet the physical and emotional needs of their members. The family is a dynamic, healthy social group that provides security and identity and allows interchange with the outside world. The family members are not so involved with each other that the separate iden tity of one is threatening to the group. But neither is the family so open that there is little sense of a shared identity.

Don Wegscheider in his book *If Only My Family Understood Me* (1979), lists some characteristics of family members in healthy families:

- the ability to negotiate with other members of the family without put-downs;

- the ability to say yes or no without the price tag of rejection;

- the ability to ask without demanding;

- the confidence in the stability of the relationship;

- the ability to show feelings of all kinds without fear of losing the relationship;

- the ability to have specific relationships with individuals in the family;

- the confidence in the honesty of the family members, in feeling trusted by others;

- the ability to celebrate, have fun and play.

There is much to celebrate and much room to grow in such families.

Dysfunctional families

A dysfunctional family has more pain and stress than it can cope with. The family system is focused on the problem behavior—in the case of a member's alcoholism, on the drinking. So much energy is expended in trying to deal with the alcoholism that family members' needs are not met or even recognized. The primary defense is denial of the problem. The resulting lack of communication and self-insulation separate family members one from another.

The signs of a dysfunctional family may be the opposite of those of a healthy family, but inconsistently so. That is, the ability to communicate, negotiate, or ask may not always be present in day-to-day living. Seemingly "good" times in an alcoholic family contrast sharply with the "bad" times. Thus the family often wavers between appearing to be functional and out-and-out-dysfunction. Inconsistencies of mood and atmosphere—on one hand dead-quiet tension, explosive anger, tears, and depression, and on the other relief and gladness—are a real puzzle for children in alcoholic families to sort out and understand. When the emotional climate of the family is unstable, the fighting and the brooding silences suggest separation or divorce to worried children.

Children also worry about the precariousness of their own and other family members' physical existence, as they wait anxiously for the sound of the car in the driveway to learn if Mom or Big Brother made it home safely without a crack-up.

The pervasive denial of the severity and extent of the problem in an alcoholic family is, as we said, an effort to deal with the pain. The denial, however, leads to a sub-set of family myths that are told and retold by children to themselves:

• We're a nice family. Nice families are not alcoholic. Therefore we can't be alcoholic.

• The alcoholism is somebody's fault. Someone is to blame. (Am I to blame?)

• If we don't talk about the problem, it doesn't exist.

• Alcoholics are bad. You shouldn't say bad things about people you love. Therefore, don't talk about your mom's or dad's drinking because somebody might think she or he is alcoholic and therefore bad.

- If we just keep doing what we're doing, things will get better somehow.

Confusion worsens with such erroneous beliefs, faulty logic, and unrealistic hopes. Our wish is that The Children's Book will help young people begin to face reality without the veil of myths.

In dysfunctional families, family rituals may also suffer. Rituals are ways of sharing meaning and identity and are the traditions that celebrate events in the life of a family—birthdays, Bar Mitzvahs, graduation parties, holidays, weekends, dinnertimes.

Drs. Steven Wolin and Linda Bennett, who studied rituals, hypothesized that the greater the change in family rituals during the time of heaviest parental drinking, the more likely would be the recurrence of alcoholism in the children's generation. Their study indicated that families who were able to protect the family rituals had the least likelihood of producing children who would become alcoholic (Aldoory, 1979). Children from alcoholic families who did *not* grow up to be alcoholics themselves had lived in families where the family rituals had been carried on *despite the behavior of the drinking parent.*

Conversely, adult alcoholics had most likely come from those families where family rituals had been neglected or dropped. Apparently, ceremonial birthday parties, Boy Scout/Girl Scout activities,

Christmas or Thanksgiving or Fourth of July traditions are important to preserve in spite of a parent's drinking. Children in alcoholic households need help in figuring out how to carry on their family rituals.

Authority and power

Families have been characterized as mother-headed (matriarchal), egalitarian, or father-headed (patriarchal) according to how power, authority, and decision-making are handled.

Power—the ability to exercise one's will over another—may be divided between sexes, between adults and children, between family members and persons from outside (from extended family, community, or workplace). Usually power is not divided democratically. Traditionally, parents have more than children, and men have had more than women. Where does the power lie in families? In alcoholic families? And how do children respond in an alcoholic family system?

1. *Parents have the power to punish and reward.* Children in an alcoholic family may learn quickly the warning signs of a parent's emotional tirade. They also learn which of their behaviors will be likely to deal with it effectively.

Children may learn that gratification of a reward should not be delayed—unless you get whatever it is you want *now*, you may not get it at all.

They may also learn that the best time to approach Dad or Mom for money is when he or she has been drinking and feels mellow and benevolent.

2. *Parents have legitimate power traditionally and automatically, simply because in most cultures the position of parent confers authority.* Children, as they grow older, may begin to rebel against the expectation that they do as parents demand just because of the parents' status.

Depending on the age of the child, drunken orders or pronouncements based on "because I say so!," if often repeated, may lose some of their ability to impress. Faced with the ineffectiveness of their own verbal commands, parents may feel justified in resorting to physically punitive methods.

3. *Parents usually have more resources than children have.* And people with the most resources—like money, possessions, or expertise—also tend to have the most power or authority. One interesting variation is Waller's (1951) "principle of least interest," which suggests that of two persons in a relationship, the one who cares least about maintaining the relationship has the most power. The person with the least interest

or concern is more apt to exploit the other and therefore has more power. Applied to an alcoholic family, the principle translates to mean that the husband or wife most concerned about maintaining the family unit has the least power. Said another way, the more the co-alcoholic members of a family try to control the drinking of the alcoholic member, the less power they will have and the greater will be the influence of alcohol and the alcoholic over family life.

4. *Alcoholism itself has power.* The erratic, inconsistent, and irresponsible behavior of an alcoholic can be a very real power in controlling others. Leaders of groups need to be aware of the drinking patterns of the alcoholics in children's homes, since the alcoholism itself determines how much and what kind of parenting children are getting.

The alcoholic may have abdicated, wholly or partially, his or her power in the family. Decisions in a family may depend more on the alcoholism than on person or situation factors.

Parenting and family roles

Parents in an alcoholic family often have been under the stress of the drinking problem for a long time. One study (Kellerman in Schneiderman, 1975) found that heavy drinking was present an average of seven years before it was identified as a problem by a family member. Because of this stress, mother and father roles are likely to be inconsistent and/or confused. The blood alcohol level of the drinking parent may have more to do with parent-child interactions than the needs of the child.

In an often seen child-parent role reversal, a child serves as caretaker for the drinking parent—sometimes for the non-drinking parent too. The child's "taking over" may lead to a pseudo maturity; the child is responsible both for herself or himself as well as for the adults in the family.

Richards (1979) pointed out that most of the literature on alcoholic families deals with the problem of male alcoholism but that there is evidence to suggest that maternal rather than paternal drinking may have more damaging consequences for the children. Drinking traditionally has been part of a masculine "he-man" sex-role stereotype, but there is no similar, culturally accepted role for women. This is one reason why the at-home woman drinker has been hard to identify and to help; problem drinking for a woman (and especially a mother) has not been regarded as acceptable behavior. Now, of course, with more women in the workplace, a woman with a drinking problem is more visible.

One major way in which children learn sex roles, how men and women behave, is by observing and copying behaviors of adults in their environment. Not enough data is available on the comparative impacts of mothers' and fathers' alcoholism on the developmental sex-role learning of boys and girls. But certainly there *are* relationships. Sex roles are the "cultural scripts" we learn as children, and in alcoholic families both drinking and non-drinking parents may present distorted role models to children. While the alcoholic, with his or her erratic and unpredictable behavior, is hardly a realistic model, neither is the non-drinking parent who models strong, silent, uncomplaining martyrdom! To the extent that either parent, drinking or not, becomes manipulative, demanding, and aggressive, these behaviors also will be watched and perhaps copied.

Other family roles have impact on children too. If the alcoholic is an older sibling, the family's energies may be centered so much around him or her that younger children may feel hurt, angry, left out, and ignored. Perhaps this relates to the fact that children who have older brothers or sisters with alcohol or drug problems sometimes follow in their footsteps and become drug-abusers themselves. They may take *their* turn at being the focus of parental anxiety! Or, on the other hand, they may shy away from drug use and try to be "perfect" to make up for the family's pain.

Children and family stress

Intense, episodic, or prolonged stress of any kind in a family causes dysfunction. Some studies have pointed out that children in alcoholic families share characteristics with children in families under other kinds of stress. Anxiety, poor concentration, low self-esteem, low self-confidence, emotional fragility—these all are characteristics of vulnerable, high-risk children from alcoholic or otherwise stressful family situations.

And remember, in summary:

• Many beliefs we hold about families are myths.

1. *"Normal" families are easily distinguished from "abnormal" ones.* Public behavior is different from private behavior. The word "normal" has a spectrum of meanings.

2. *Differences of opinion within a family are always harmoniously settled.* Alcoholic families may not have learned how to handle conflict well. Unfortunately, children learn poor lessons from watching and listening to adults fighting and arguing. The impact of such discord is different for each child since each lives in a somewhat "different" family.

3. *Communication within a family is always natural and easy.* Denial of reality, no-win messages and double binds, ignoring, and mislabeling are commonly found in families in which communication is a problem (and certainly alcoholic families fall into this category). Children living in such families will need practice and time to express thoughts and feelings. Just talking may be very hard for them.

4. *The typical "right" kind of family has remained an ideal for generations. Now these families are breaking apart.* There probably never was an "ideal" family in the past. Children have grown up successfully in many different kinds of families. Alcoholism is not the result of divorce or of any one single factor, functional or structural. There may not be a single "typical" alcoholic family.

5. *There are "good" parents and "bad" parents.* Parents seldom can be classified sharply in these ways. Different kinds of children bring out different kinds of parenting styles and behaviors. An alcoholic parent is likely to be less sensitive to the needs of the children because of the enormity of the family's alcohol-related prob-

lems. Resulting inconsistencies are hard for children to understand.

6. *What goes on in other people's families is no one else's business.* In an alcoholic family, children are vulnerable and are not likely to be offered help from within the family. Help must come from concerned persons outside.

- Functional families differ in some important ways from dysfunctional ones. Dysfunctional, alcoholic families trip over their own sub-set of myths, which block communication. Family rituals are important for the cohesion and identity of a family.

- Power and authority often are handled differently in an alcoholic family than in a non-alcoholic one. Power, best shared by mother and father, is not likely to be balanced equitably in an alcoholic family.

- Family roles may be confused within an alcoholic family, especially mother and father roles. Some research indicates that the effect of an alcoholic mother may be worse for the family than that of an alcoholic father. Children may assume parental roles and responsibilities.

Chapter Three
Children and Change

If someone were asked to choose the best years of the lifespan, they might well choose middle childhood—the years between eight and twelve. It is easy, as an adult, to call up the nostalgic smell of freshly-cut grass or of library paste, the hubbub of the school cafeteria or playground, the warmth of nuzzling puppies, the taste of chocolate chip cookie batter or ice cream or peanut butter sandwiches.

The memories of a child who grew up in an alcoholic family may include some of these. But there probably are other recollections too: loud, angry voices late at night, the sharp smell of whiskey or the sour smell of emptied beer cans, a parent sprawled on a couch, the screech of tires as the family car turns into the driveway or the silence, the waiting, the tension when it doesn't. Memories also might include excuses to friends, ("I can't have you over tonight, my mom's sick."), parental promises that weren't kept and, for one twelve-year-old girl, the box of crayons and coloring book (more appropriate for a child half her age) that were a birthday gift from a mother who had forgotten which birthday this was. Happy and awful times are mixed in a jumbled, seesaw pattern—doubtless somewhat different from family to family. The child of an alcoholic or drug dependent parent finds that behaviors praised one day are ignored in stony silence or met by apathetic withdrawal the next.

The massive denial of the problem in an alcoholic family results in the three messages that Claudia Black (1981) suggests these children receive, "Don't talk. Don't trust. Don't feel." Talking, trusting, or feeling probably have not been much help to the child in the past and may have gotten her or him into trouble. In a children's group, understanding and patience are needed by the leader and other members while children try to talk and hesitatingly attempt to allow themselves to feel and trust.

Sam, a nine-year-old whose father was in treatment for alcoholism, was having trouble sharing his feelings with his father and the rest of the family in counseling sessions. During one session while Sam's sister was talking about some of her painful feelings, Sam ran out of the room, down three flights of stairs and out of the building. The counselor followed, struggling to keep up with the obviously upset boy. Finally Sam stopped, turned to the counselor, and yelled, "I try really, really hard to keep my feelings all locked up inside me—like in a metal box with a great big chain wrapped around it and a big padlock. And *you* ...you want me to let them all out!" The inconsistency and unpredictability of the family, coupled with the unspoken rules about "not talking," present a complicated set of demands that often result in a dilemma for a child like Sam.

A child's resources change with each year of growth. But while there are age-related predictabilities in physical, cognitive, and social areas of a child's development, not all these facets of development appear evenly in a given child or in children of the same age. In all of these areas, however, a child's self-esteem is tested over and over again in the process of growing up.

Diane, eleven, is tall for her age and looks older than she is. Adults treat her as though she were older, and her height helps her excel on the basketball team. Since Diane's mother is alcoholic, much of Diane's self-concept and self-esteem reflect what her coach and other members of her team feel about her. Her dad attends as many of the games as he can too.

Joel, ten, isn't very good at sports but gets fairly good grades. Joel's father tends to drink heavily on weekends, at which times Joel's mother focuses her attention on her husband and just getting through these rough days. Joel's grandmother lives in town, however, and he spends as much weekend time as he can with her. She and Joel go out to movies and museums and art exhibits, and Joel is developing a fund of information about ancient Egypt.

Both Diane and Joel are finding new ways to define their self-concept and to find routes around the family problems. Some children may not be so fortunate. They may need help to identify their options and encouragement to begin this kind of rerouting or "map-making."

Both individual growth and family change take place within a cultural context. With rapid societal and technological changes in our civilization, stress may be the inevitable accompaniment. Concern has been expressed (Elkind, 1982) that one group feeling stress, the children, is being "hurried" into adulthood. Clothing styles, cosmetics, music, and language all give children the idea that the status of childhood is greatly inferior to the status of adulthood. The incessant beat of advertising messages give children reason to believe that "adult" behavior, including sexual activity and drug use, is to be admired and copied. Children from alcoholic families may be more vulnerable to this kind of hurry-and-grow-up siren song, since the reality of their own childhoods and family situations is painful. These children already may have had to carry out adult responsibilities in caring for household or siblings and have therefore entered a pseudo-adulthood.

If growth is so multifaceted and the societal messages are so compelling, what do children need to keep their balance as they grow? First of all, they need to be allowed to be children. They need to develop skills and talents that provide self-esteem now and that build a foundation for the future. They also need to be valued by their families and a few special people outside the family, to develop the ability to make decisions and evaluate their outcomes, to give and receive affection, to develop empathy and social concern for others. Finally, they need time and support as they fit the pieces of their lives together.

The following sections will summarize in more detail general areas of development: 1) physical growth and maturation; 2) cognitive change including language, memory, and moral development, and 3) the acquisition of social skills related to friends and family.

Physical growth and maturation

Between the ages of eight and twelve, a child's body changes rapidly. Height and weight increase. Control of large muscles is nearly complete, enabling the child to participate in a variety of physical games. Children also gain more control over small muscles, so skill and dexterity improve. These changes in children's bodies may occur rapidly enough so as to impart a new sense of mastery over the environment, and may be part of the reason children in the middle years are frequently so optimistic about the future.

Children from alcoholic families may be encouraged by their newly acquired physical competence, yet confused and frustrated by the inability of these new-found skills to change a family environment that is emotionally inadequate. Girls and boys are nearly the same height between eight and twelve, although the growth spurt for girls at the end of this period enables them to outstrip their male age-mates in height and weight. There is an average difference of about two years in the timing of the growth spurt—probably causing acute embarassment for some children. At a period when peer approval is so important, children find it uncomfortable to be either precocious or slow in physical development.

Self-concept is involved with physical development; the shape of the physical "container" influences a child's interaction both with children and with adults. How children feel about themselves is influenced by the reactions of others to their relative attractiveness, stature, strength, overweight or underweight, and other physical differences. Families and parents are often the ones who note physical characteristics of which to be proud ("You're built just like your father! He could run well, too."). They can also buffer a child's disappointment when physical skills or characteristics fall short ("So you won't be on the football team...other sports are more challenging, I think."). Alcoholic families may be too dysfunctional to provide this kind of buffering or translating for children, so the children may be left to make what sense they can of physiological information about themselves.

Fetal Alcohol Syndrome

For some children whose mothers drank alcohol during pregnancy, the family problems may be multiplied by the group of symptoms mentioned earlier—Fetal Alcohol Syndrome (FAS) or Fetal Alcohol Effects (FAE). FAS, officially identified in 1973, is the third most common neurological birth defect (Robe, 1982). FAS experts estimate that one out of every six hundred to one thousand newborns has FAS and that anywhere from eleven to seventy-six percent of children of alcoholic mothers are born with one or more of its symptoms. Fetal Alcohol Effects may include small size, abnormally small head, slowed mental development, facial characteristics that can include a flattish appearance in profile, narrow slit-like eyes, flat cheeks, and a short upturned nose. Other symptoms may include other deformities such as heart murmurs, malformation of fingers or toes, hip dislocation, kidney/genital problems, and hernias, and/or muscular problems. As FAS children grow they may show evidence of hyperactivity with possible mental retardation, behavior problems in school, and an underweight, skinny physique.

Any professional dealing with children of alcoholic mothers should be aware that such handicaps are possible.

Although it has not yet been adequately researched, Frank Seixas, M.D., former medical director of the National Council on Alcoholism, said in 1977: "The possibility of these children having a triple load of potentiality for alcoholism is great. Namely, the possible genetic effect, plus the infant metabolism changes, and the social effects of having to live with an alcoholic mother." (*Just So It's Healthy,* Robe, 1982, p. 24).

Cognitive changes

Cognitive changes have to do with thinking, language, memory, attention, and moral reasoning. ·

Thinking

There are interrelated changes in the kinds of thoughts children are capable of as they grow older. Piaget (Flavell, 1977) has outlined four general stages:

Age	Stage	Focus
0-2	Sensorimotor	Focus is on the coordination of senses and actions.
2-7	Preoperational	Thinking is dominated by perceptions and images. How things look is how things are.
7-11	Concrete Operations	Thinking is dominated by logic, but logic that is limited to the real and concrete. Thought is entrenched in the here and now. Two concepts can be handled at one time.
11-12+	Formal Operations	Children can think abstractly, about hypothetical situations. "If...then" thought is possible.

The thinking of very young children at the beginning of elementary school typically is egocentric and *dominated by the way things appear to be.* Clouds, for example, may be thought to "be alive" because they move across the sky. As children grow older, they are not as bound by the purely perceptual point of view but are still struggling with the problem of how things appear to be and how they really are.

Children of seven through eleven or so are tied to the tangible and concrete, are literal in their interpretations of reality, and are still limited by the "here and now." Although Mary, ten, whose family was in treatment because her father was alcoholic, had been told repeatedly by both her parents and the counselor that she was not responsible for her father's alcoholism, she was not convinced. Finally the counselor asked her what she thought she had done to cause the alcoholism. Mary replied, "Well, alcohol causes alcoholism doesn't it? I used to make my dad's drinks, so I must have made him into an alcoholic." When it was explained to her that alcohol doesn't cause alcoholism, and that she had only been following her father's orders, Mary was relieved of her burden of guilt.

Seven-to-eleven-year-olds are egocentric and tend to see everything in relation to themselves. When bad or confusing things happen—such as alcoholism in the family—the children blame themselves. Adult leaders must realize how important it is to let children know that parents' alcoholism *is not their fault.* However, just *telling* them that they are not to blame is not always enough. With the help of The Children's Book and the group, an adult leader needs to listen and follow a child's line of reasoning to its conclusion in an effort to discern why she or he thinks this way and to interrupt the faulty logic.

Besides changing their view of reality, children mature in their ability to classify, to group, and to place in order. A preschool-aged child's "collection" of things in a box may contain a button, a baseball card, a rock found last summer, and a half-eaten candy bar. There is little rhyme or reason to this kind of collection except that these are the things children "want to keep." "That's good stuff," a child may howl as a mother threatens to throw it out. An elementary-aged child, however, is more likely to collect stamps, comic books, autographs, statues of unicorns, friendship pins, or other categorized mementos. This newly-minted power to group and classify may be related to the tendency of some children to become temporary braggards about what they can do and how much they know. The imposition of personal will upon an assortment of objects produces a powerful "in control" feeling.

The power to group and classify can pertain to people as well as objects. Children try to separate the "good guys" from the "bad guys." Old western movies used white hats, white shirts, white horses, and clean-shaven faces to help young audiences identify the good guys and make the distinction. Children in alcoholic families can benefit from being able, at this age, to explore the distinction between an alcoholic as a "sick guy" instead of a "bad guy."

Rigid "good-bad" categories and stereotypes are the result of classification, and children can be as hard on themselves as they are on others. Being too short, too heavy, too clumsy — or too anything — can cause problems for children. Self-esteem and self-worth come, in part, from belonging in or not belonging in certain kinds of categories. Adults must listen carefully in order to hear on what bases children are making their distinctions and judgments.

Elementary-aged children are literal thinkers. They have difficulty thinking abstractly and dealing effectively with hypothetical situations. Instead, they usually are concerned with real objects and situations, or with those that are easily imagined or have been directly experienced in the past.

John, nine, talked about hiding behind the couch and keeping watch on his parents while they argued. When the counselor asked John why he had done this, he said that he watched and listened and tried to figure out who was right, who was wrong, and whose fault it was. He listened, too, to see if they were arguing about him. He hoped to find out if it had been his fault. John seemed to feel that it would help his own situation if he could, detective-like, figure out what the "real problem" was. Reality, of course, does not usually resolve itself into a single, simple "problem." But children like John can benefit greatly from listening to and talking with other children from alcoholic homes.

Language

Children's increased cognitive skills are reflected in accompanying language competence. By age eight, almost all children understand the syntax and grammar of their native language and can use this language adeptly.

Elementary school children begin to understand metaphors and delight in jokes and riddles involving ambiguities and double meanings of words. Humor is recognized as an important aspect of mental health. Feeling secure is related to the ability to appreciate humor, and humor is a way to deal with situations that might be worrisome or anxiety-provoking. Humor is used in social skills too—just knowing the current, popular jokes may be an indicator of acceptance and security within the social groups at school.

Many children in alcoholic homes may have had little experience in humor or play. A few have yet to know the freedom of telling a joke, erupting into laughter, or collapsing in a fit of giggles. This experience is a worthy objective for young children of alcoholics, and the group may provide the needed security for children to react freely to a joke or a funny story.

Children of this age use language as a way of mastering and organizing their world. Language helps them suggest ideas, make complicated requests and inquiries, and share their inner world of feelings and dreams. Communicating gives children a sense of power when they see their words influence the actions, feelings, and ideas of those around them.

An important note: Children's language is often different from adult language, since children delight in making up brand-new words. And words used both by children and by adults may have special meanings for children. Concepts and sub-concepts may also appear differently to adults and children. One father, as his seven-year-old sped down the hall, reminded his son that he had been repeatedly told not to run in the house. His son looked up at him, surprised, and sputtered, "But I wasn't running, I was galloping!" Some parents would see this as a verbal affront to adult authority, as "talking back," but for a child, this is a totally logical distinction. A wise parent will say something like, "Oh, I understand. There is a difference, but galloping makes noise too and your little sister is napping."

The literal thinking of the mid-years child extends to "bad" language and "dirty words." One child was upset over the language she heard her mother using when she was drunk. (The family usually had strong prohibitions about the kind of language children used.) "All those dirty words will stick in my head and I'm not supposed to use them!" she sobbed. "What will I do if one gets out?" The "getting-out" implies that words have a power of their own to hurt—an idea that has been called "word realism." Word realism also shows itself in the "magic words," the chants, the rituals, the passwords that children use. Even adults have words to express strong emotions or to invoke the powers that be to intercede.

Children who believe in the power of words also are apt to believe in their accuracy. A child who is called ugly names by a drinking parent is likely to believe that those names really do describe him or her. Children aren't skilled or practiced yet in looking at others' states of mind or ascertaining possible motives. This is why teasing and name-calling can have such powerful negative effects. On the other hand, as an example of the positive power of language, the words in the "diploma" (at the back of The Children's Book) awarded at the end of the group sessions will be prized!

Memory and attention

By age eight, children can remember back several years. Most of the research on memory in children this age has been confined to the memory for words, objects, or patterns. Since younger children perceive differently than do older children, they retain information differently as well. An inter-personal situation is apt to be interpreted one way by a younger child and another by an older child. One factor remains constant, however. Like John, as he listened behind the couch, *a child always interprets circumstances in relation to himself.* He may have thought *he* was the reason for a disagreement, or for the drinking. The group experience can help children remember, examine, and "defuse" unpleasant memories and feelings—once they understand that their parents were sick and irresponsible at that time.

Children are always most likely to select out and pay attention to what they think is interesting. By the middle elementary years, their ability to screen out background noises and distractions has improved so they can focus on what interests them. They are most likely to pay attention to someone else if that person is like them in age, sex, or other identifiable characteristics. This is one good reason for working with children of alcoholics in a group setting. A group can help children realize that their problems are not unique. They can benefit from hearing how others their age cope with similar problems.

Adults leading a children's group may worry about children's lack of attention. But lack of attention can be a symptom. It can mean that children are uncomfortable at that moment, or that whatever is going on may be unclear and need focus, or that a short break is needed for standing and stretching. The task of the leader is to try to figure out what the behavior really means.

Moral reasoning

A young child is likely to see right and wrong, morality and justice, punishment and crime very differently from an older one. Kohlberg (1976) has described three levels of development; each with two stages. They are outlined briefly below:

Preconventional Level	*Emphasis*
Stage 1.	Punishment and obedience orientation. Children obey the rules of others to avoid punishment.
Stage 2.	Instrumental exchange. Children follow rules only when it is to their advantage. Right is what is "fair," meaning an equal exchange, a deal, an agreement.
Conventional Level	
Stage 3.	Good-boy, nice-girl orientation. Children want to please other people, to be considered "good" by those whose opinions count. Being "good" involves having good motives, showing concern for others. They are developing their own ideas of what a "good" person is.

Stage 4.   System-maintaining orientation.
              Concern is for carrying out the
              duties that are your obligation.
              Laws are to be obeyed, ("What if
              everybody did it?") Children are
              concerned for maintaining the
              social order.

Postconventional Level

Stage 5.   Social-contract orientation. They
              think about society's welfare and
              value the will of the majority.
              There is an awareness that
              people hold a variety of values
              and opinions and that there is a
              possibility of conflict. The
              Golden Rule.

Stage 6.   Universal-ethical-principles
              orientation. People act in
              accordance with internalized
              standards. Mother Theresa,
              Gandhi, and Martin Luther King
              are all examples of people who
              exhibited Stage 6 belief systems.

Moral reasoning is closely related to growth in cognitive development. Younger school-age children tend to see things as right or wrong, with no ambiguities and no allowance for intentions. Acts are judged by their results with little appreciation for different points of view or extenuating circumstances. Children in alcoholic families who are in Stage 1 will probably accept the punishment-and-obedience orientation. An abused child may explain to a social worker that "Mommy *had* to punish me because I was bad." Children who are operating in the Stage 2 area (following rules if the rules are to their advantage) find inconsistencies in their alcoholic family that they can't seem to understand. Things may not always be according to "what is fair."

Stages 3 and 4 in the development of moral reasoning depend on reinforcement by persons in the child's environment inside and outside the home. For children living in an alcoholic family, reinforcements may be more closely related to moods of adult family members than to a child's behaviors. If the desire to please is met with inattention or casual neglect, the child may either redouble efforts or decide that efforts are futile and give up altogether. Children in Stage 4 may work hard to fulfill what they perceive to be the expectations of society. They've been described as "superkids" or "heroes." Some children in alcoholic families have expressed the expectation that trying harder and achieving more will cause the alcoholism to stop. An adult may have a hard time convincing a child that the world doesn't work this way. "Superkid" and other roles that children may assume are explained more fully in Chapter Four. A group of children, talking together, can provide support for exploring these roles and their attendant expectations.

Researchers point out that not all human beings reach the highest stages of moral reasoning (5 and 6). In fact, there is currently some discussion as to exactly what these highest stages entail. Stages 5 and 6 imply that conduct is now controlled by internalized principles. There is the realization that people hold different and sometimes conflicting values, and behavior is now interpreted by attempting to understand underlying motives and reasons. A son or daughter who understands and accepts the behavior of an alcoholic mother or father as being part of a disease process not directly controlled by the parent has made great strides toward this level of moral development. Perhaps when we can understand and forgive our parents for their "mistakes" in our upbringing, we are moving toward our own maturity.

Social skills

Roles within the family

The social world of children depends, in large part, on other people's reactions to them: reactions based on age, sex, size, and other characteristics.

Whether children are oldest, youngest, middle, or only children are factors which also seem to play an important role. People have long been interested in the effects of birth order. Galton noted years ago (1896) that there was a preponderance of firstborn children among eminent scientists in Britain. Newsweek (1969) reported that five of the seven original astronauts were firstborns and the remaining two were "only" children. Earlier research on firstborns (Koch, 1955) suggested that they are apt to be more articulate, do better in school, be more responsible and better planners. Others point out that firstborns have more opportunity to interact with adults and therefore are treated in a more "grown-up" fashion by the adult world. The firstborn is also the only child to have "lost" his or her reigning position when a new baby comes along. The firstborn is the only one to have "broken in" a set of brand-new parents. The achievements of the firstborn may be more likely to be met with astonishment, pride, worry and hovering concern than those of subsequent children.

The "oldest child" role in alcoholic families has been described by those who have worked with these children. Claudia Black (1979) called the older child the Responsible One, and pointed out that the maturity and responsibility asked of this child in an alcoholic family resulted in the early loss of a "childhood." Sharon Wegscheider (1979) called the oldest child the Family Hero, emphasizing that many of these children seem to have succeeded admirably *in spite of* their unpredictable and chaotic families. She adds that both the drinking and non-drinking parents see this oldest child as a symbol that all is well in the family. The apparent success of the child adds to the family's already present system of denial of the drinking problem. Don Wegscheider, in writing about family roles in a crisis (1979), calls this the Caretaker role. The Caretaker realizes that his or her success brings comfort and joy both to the drinking and to the non-drinking parent. Paradoxically, however, since the family situation never improves, the oldest child also feels inadequate and guilty because he or she has been unable to change things.

Although there are slightly differing emphases on this oldest-child theme from these three therapists, all three tell us that adult years are hard for these children who have had to mature so quickly. Some may find another adult to "care for." For example, an oldest daughter may marry an alcoholic. These children may grow to be adults who are hard workers and who prize success but are at risk for stress-related problems. They are adept at handling other people's problems but are not aware of their own needs. Sharon Wegscheider suggests that Heroes often enter "caretaking" professions—like nursing, counseling, or the ministry—and that they are at risk for professional "burn-out" unless they can develop some insight and self-understanding. In a group of children, the leader or facilitator should be aware that the mature-appearing child who holds himself or

herself slightly apart from the group may be a
family hero trying to deal with feelings of in-
adequacy or guilt.

The world of the youngest child contrasts dra-
matically with that of the oldest. The youngest is
likely to be more flexible, adaptable, and socially
adept than the oldest brother or sister. The no
longer first-time parents may be more tolerant,
less demanding, more accomodating to the wishes
of the "baby of the family." This role in alcoholic
families is called the Mascot by Sharon Wegscheider and the Family Pet by Don Wegscheider.
The Family Pet is the attention-getter whose humor and cuteness hide her or his fears. The
clowning distracts family members from the alcoholism. Children in this role may appear hyperactive, have trouble sitting still or concentrating.

In one session of a children's group, the longer
the discussion remained on what it felt like to live
in a family where drinking was a problem, the
more Mary Ann made faces, grasped her throat
and pretended to die. Her behavior grew more
distracting and frantic as her anxiety apparently
increased. A leader can introduce a physical activity for a few minutes to interrupt this sequence, or
acknowledge verbally that some things are hard to
talk about while sitting still. Role-playing can be
helpful too, especially with younger children. Family Pets are easy to spot in a group. Although they
seem to be inattentive, leaders should be aware

that their behavior masks their fears as they try to keep the focus on superficialities.

Remember too that, whereas older siblings may remember other happier times, the youngest child is born into a family whose behavior and communication may have been dysfunctional all his or her life. Therefore, the present is the only reality the youngest knows.

Research is sketchy on "middle" children. Some work suggests that families tend to be not as attentive to middle children as to their oldest and youngest. Middle children may look to the oldest brother or sister as a model to admire or identify with. But they also use this model for comparison, to figure out how they themselves are different.

In alcoholic families some middle children appear to "give up" and not try to intervene while others act out their frustrations. The child who gives up has been called the Forgotten Child by Don Wegscheider, the Lost Child by Sharon Wegscheider, and the Adjuster by Claudia Black. These children apparently learn to deal with their feelings of helplessness by withdrawing—sometimes into a fantasy world—and becoming like small, quiet mice watching the family situation from the periphery. Loneliness is the price paid for escaping the family's tension and discord. The Adjuster is detached and concentrates on simply getting along, putting up with and adjusting to the situation.

Other "middle children" in alcoholic families may act out anger, defiance, and conflict, especially in school, where anti-adult, anti-authority behavior gains attention. This child has been described as a Problem Child by Don Wegscheider, as Acting-out by Claudia Black and as a Scapegoat by Sharon Wegscheider. When there is a Scapegoat, the family has someone other than the alcoholic to blame for its troubles. This child absorbs the family's disappointment and anger. Scapegoats or Problem Children may be aware of their anger but not very aware of their other feelings. According to Claudia Black, these Problem/Acting-out Children may begin using alcohol and/or other drugs at an early age—which may, of course, exacerbate their psychosocial problems.

Remember that one child can combine elements of all of these roles, depending on the level of conflict at home, the child's success or failure in attempting to reduce the family dissonance, and what is happening outside the home—at school, with teachers, or with friends. Children will create their own roles, their scripts and scenarios out of their own perception of reality. They will try to control what they feel they can control—through achieving (the Hero), clowning (the Family Pet), or living up to the bad behavior expected of them through negative achievement (the Problem Child). If they feel they have no control or effect, that matters are out of their hands, their logical response will be a detached, avoiding, or placating role (the Adjuster).

One goal of the group experience is to help children perceive that they *can* be more in control of those parts of their lives where control is possible—to help them develop, as the Serenity Prayer says, "the courage to change the things" they can.

Friendships

Social learning also takes place through friendships. Self-concept and self-esteem may be enhanced or weakened by the presence or absence of friends. Children in the beginning years of school form friendships on different bases than do older children. Often early friends are made because of proximity or shared interests. Mollie and Sandie in the third grade are friends because they both like to play "Barbies" and because they live next door. They like each other and enjoy doing things together. As Mollie and Sandie grow, however, friendship may mean more—being "best friends" and intensely loyal to each other. By the age of nine, friendships are important for sharing problems and for mutual support. Children now understand that friends can help deal with feelings of sadness or loneliness.

Who are the popular children—the ones with the most friends? Children tend to choose friends who look good to them and who are of their own sex. Physical attractiveness is a great asset. Studies indicate that "popular" children are more adept at managing conflict, taking another person's point of view, and cooperating and sharing. Some researchers have attempted to change the behavior of unpopular children, and the results have been encouraging. Unpopular children need help in understanding how their behavior affects other children.

The development of social skills may be thwarted for a child in an alcoholic family who may have difficulty in finding a "safe" time to invite friends over. He or she may also be at a social disadvantage if physically neglected because of a parent's drinking. Stringy and unwashed hair, dirty or funny clothes certainly can interfere with social relationships or friendships, and therefore with self-esteem. Friends provide windows through which children glimpse homes and family lives different from their own. The comparisons may be more puzzling than enlightening since "normal" family life, as we said earlier, may not have been part of the child's experience. And, of course, school provides an arena for testing—over and over again—social as well as academic success.

Teachers need to be able to recognize that withdrawn shy children, acting-out children, and overly mature achievers all may be reflecting drug-using or drinking troubles at home. School counselors and teachers have expressed the need for more information about alcoholism and other drug dependency, especially for ways to work this kind of information into existing curricula. (A list of resources is given on page 126.)

And remember, in summary:

1. Children *are* aware of what is going on in their environment. They attach whatever meanings and interpretations that their ages, capabilities, and experiences dictate.

2. Children in alcoholic families are standing on two planes of change: the first is the growth and maturation of their own bodies and capabilities, and the second plane, much more unstable, is the unpredictability of their own families. It is as though one foot is on a surface that is slowly moving forward while the other, badly balanced, is on an uneven and rocky incline.

3. Fetal Alcohol Syndrome (FAS) children are likely to have special and severe difficulties in development.

4. Growth is complex and many-faceted. All aspects of development do not follow the same timetable. A child may appear much more mature than his or her contemporar-

ies because of earlier physical development, but emotions and cognition do not necessarily follow suit.

5. Children understand their world through thought processes that are different from (not inferior to) adult thinking. The thinking of a seven-to-twelve-year-old is apt to be concrete and literal, which may lead to conclusions that are erroneous.

6. Language is important in that it organizes ideas and gives children a sense of power and mastery. The alcoholic family rules about not talking make the expression of feelings difficult for children. The group leader can make a child more comfortable through universalizing, like this: "Many children in a situation like that would have felt pretty scared," rather than, "You must have felt pretty scared. Do you want to tell us about it?" The "many children" approach does not push the child to express emotions through language.

7. The classification skills of an elementary-aged child's cognitive development lead him or her to form social categories or stereotypes. Since these categories may not be duplicates of adult classification, the group may explore similarities and differ-

ences between adults' and children's views. For instance, "drinking," "drunk," "alcoholic" may have different meanings for children and adults.

8. Similarly, language is used differently by a child. Teasing and name-calling are apt to be taken quite literally.

9. Moral development, the sense of right and wrong, is closely tied to cognitive development. Elementary-aged children may be concerned with being "good," pleasing people by doing what they are supposed to do.

10. Birth order has a strong influence on the roles that children adopt within a family. Firstborn roles in an alcoholic family have been described as the Responsible One, the Family Hero, the Caretaker. Youngest roles have been dubbed the Mascot or Family Pet. Other roles, often middle-child roles, are the Forgotten Child, Lost Child, Adjuster for children who have withdrawn from the family struggle and given up, or the Problem Child, Acting-out, Scapegoat for the defiant, angry, anti-authority children who thus express the family's turmoil. Of course, roles in real life often are not as clear as these descriptions. Also, a child

can exhibit elements of several different roles.

11. Children's friendships differ with age. By nine or ten, children have learned to depend on friendships for emotional support, not just shared interests.

12. All who work with children should become sensitized to the visible as well as the invisible signals that indicate the presence of an "ELEPHANT in the living room." Many school systems and teachers have recognized the need to give a priority to learning about children and alcoholism.

Chapter Four
Helping Children of Alcoholics

The Elephant in the Living Room: The Children's Book and The Leader's Guide for Helping Children of Alcoholics were developed because staff in alcoholism treatment centers and in elementary and middle schools wanted a way to begin addressing the needs of children in alcoholic families. The Children's Book and Leader's Guide were designed to assist them in setting up support groups for these children. These support groups can provide not only education about alcoholism/chemical dependency, but the opportunity to discuss the problems these children are experiencing.

The Children's Book was designed for use in alcoholism treatment centers, in children's support groups sponsored by mental health agencies or voluntary organizations, and in elementary and middle schools. Leaders need to consider how the differences in settings may affect the use of The Children's Book. The potential group leader should read all of this chapter, since some questions, such as the need for parental consent, may become an issue in your setting.

In alcoholism treatment centers

Some programs treat only the alcoholic. Some programs involve family members and significant others in educational lectures and seminars. An increasing number of programs include marital and family counseling as an integral part of the treatment process.

Whatever the type of treatment program, some generalizations can be made about the use of these materials and the children's reactions to them. Since the alcoholic has made the move to become involved in a treatment program, an important change has taken place in the family. Efforts are being made to confront and accept a more realistic view of the drinking and the consequences. The family *is* beginning to acknowledge the "ELEPHANT in the living room." Parents still may deny that the children have been affected adversely by the alcoholism and not want a child to participate in a group. However there is a greater likelihood that parents will permit their children to participate if staff members strongly recommend it as important for the child and the family in the treatment process.

Children's reactions to their parents' or siblings' participation in the alcoholism treatment program should be considered. Because their initial reactions may be denial, fear, confusion, (about why they or their parents are involved in treatment), as well as relief, children need to be given the opportunity to discuss their feelings and have their questions answered at the first group meeting.

Initially, children may have trouble talking about the alcohol problem since the family rule until now has been "Don't talk about the drinking." They will need to establish trust with the group leaders and members.

Some children may be intimidated by a treatment program located in a hospital or clinic setting, equating it with shots, surgery, and other painful experiences. Their fears may be reduced if they can see the patients' rooms and learn what kinds of activities patients participate in during treatment. Also, children usually feel more comfortable if there are books, games, or toys available to them in the waiting room or in a special children's group room.

Children can be an invaluable part of the treatment process. Because children frequently are the most honest members about the role drinking has played in the family, they can add essential information to break through the family's denial of the alcoholism. With encouragement, children can express effectively the pain and anguish that the drinking and resulting behavior have caused them. Although an alcoholic may be able to deny or block recognition of a spouse's pain, attributing it to other marital or personal problems, he or she will find it more difficult to ignore the pain of a young child who wants only the love and protection of a parent. A family's concern for the safety and well-being of a child can be a strong motivator for change and recovery in the family.

However it is vitally important, in fact, critical, for a counselor to keep a child from becoming too much the focus and agent of a family's change. *Children are not the cause nor the cure for their parents' alcoholism.* To make a child the main focus of an intervention or treatment process is to burden the child with unrealistic expectations and responsibilities. This can only reinforce a child's feelings of guilt, blame, and powerlessness if the parent's treatment is not successful. It also reinforces the child's erroneous belief that life can only improve if the parent stops drinking.

In general children's support groups

Some mental health agencies and voluntary organizations or fellowships offer support groups for children. Although some support groups are specifically for children of alcoholics, many groups are more general. If the support group is for children from families with a variety of problems, but not exclusively alcoholism, leaders may modify some of the activities. In this case, the leaders should present information and activities in an educational and non-threatening way, which allows children of alcoholics to talk about family drinking if they wish but does not single them out. Since the workbook activities are designed to help children improve self-esteem and decision-making and problem-solving skills, many of the activities could be helpful to children whether or not alcoholism is the problem in their families.

Prior to children's participation in the group, it is usually a good idea to inform the parents of the content of the workbook, offer them the opportunity to voice their concerns over the material and give informed consent to their child's participation. If alcoholism is a problem in the family, the parent may not recognize—or may minimize—the effects the alcoholism has had on the child. However leaders should remember that the parent does at least recognize that the child is experiencing problems and is taking the positive step of seeking help for the child. In each case, the child's needs should be addressed first, both for the child's sake and because this is a good way to begin to develop the trust of the parent.

Parents should be informed that since alcoholism is being discussed as a part of the children's group activities, a child may question the role of drinking in the family. A child may challenge the family's typical ways of coping with the drinking behavior. Parents should be encouraged to discuss any concerns about this with the leader. The leader then can urge the parents to seek information and/or help for themselves through AA, Al-Anon, or other support or counseling services. Parents may be anxious about what their children have said or may say about them in the group. While confidentiality is important, leaders can help reduce a parent's anxiety by explaining the general activities of each session either before or after the group. Also, it is sometimes helpful to have an informal get-together with parents and children (a pizza party or ice cream social or movie) so that parents can interact with leaders and other parents in a more relaxed environment.

In school settings

The school setting presents a unique and challenging opportunity for helping children in alcoholic families since all children are required to attend school. Although approximately four to six children in a classroom of twenty-five (Korcok, 1981) live in families in which alcoholism is a problem, many of these children are not identified as children of alcoholics. Some may speak up about their problems after or during alcohol and drug education presentations. Others may be identified by teachers, counselors, or other staff members. The book *Broken Bottles, Broken Dreams* by Charles Deutsch offers suggestions on how to identify children of alcoholics in schools by using alcohol education programs and teacher in-service training programs.

Once these children are identified as needing help, the question arises as to what kind and how much help can be given to them by teachers and counselors, especially if prior permission is not obtained from parents or guardians. Although involvement and support of parents is important, given the strong denial of the problem by family members as well as the alcoholic, it is not always reasonable to expect parental consent. This raises many ethical, moral, and legal concerns for which there are no concrete or easy answers.

Many professionals have stated that children of alcoholics will not receive what they need if they have to wait for parental acknowledgment of the alcoholism and permission to participate in a program of help. Knowing the risks to the children of doing nothing, many teachers and counselors feel a responsibility to provide these children with help and guidance.

Legally, the question of what kinds of services can be provided to children without prior parental permission is a confusing one. Most legal cases involving lack of parental consent in providing services to children have pertained to medical and surgical situations. There are no clear-cut legal definitions of what constitutes malpractice or liability in counseling or in nonphysical treatment.

McCabe, in his paper "Children in Need: Consent Issues in Treatment" (1977), states:

> Everyone who deals with specific situations has to be able to judge the individual risks. Sometimes the calculated risk wins, but it must be recognized for what it is. Future trends are important in calculating a risk. The law in regards to family relationships is old and tenacious, however, and that too must be considered. Anyone who deals with children's problems is, therefore, advised to proceed with caution when parental disfavor may be threatened. (p. 4)

Another confusing, related question is: "What constitutes treatment?" How does treatment differ from education and support? It has long been the province of teachers and school counselors to provide their students with education about a variety of topics and to give them support and guidance in their emotional development. The activities in the children's workbook of *An Elephant in the Living Room* are designed to provide education about alcoholism and suggestions for coping with a variety of problems. Use of The Children's Book in a group setting is intended to help facilitate emotional growth and development. Whether or not this would be considered "treatment" in a legal sense would ultimately depend on the way in which the book and activities were used and a judgment in a court of law as to whether or not this use constituted "treatment" requiring prior parental consent.

The likelihood that a parent would take a teacher or counselor to court over this issue is probably slim, since most families entrenched in the denial of the alcoholism and the covering up of its consequences are not going to embroil themselves in a legal battle that would only draw attention to the situation.

Deutsch states:

> In summary, the law fails to provide clear ground rules for when treatment without parental consent is justified and when it is an infringement of rights. Given recent legal trends, the nature of the illness, and a remediation process that is essentially educative and supportive, there seems to be legal basis for assuming that consent and adequate disclosure are not required for adolescents but must be obtained for younger children. The crucial safeguard for nonclinical helping institutions, such as schools, is community support rather than explicit legal dictums. In some locales intervention as well as treatment might be viewed as an encroachment on parental rights. In the absence of ironclad legal grounds, the active support of respected elements in the community becomes even more vital. (p. 163)

Whether or not a legal liability is involved, the importance of administrative support and backing cannot be overstated. Most principals, when confronted by an angry parent, will back up a teacher's or counselor's actions if they have been a part of the initial decision to help a child and are apprised ahead of time of a potentially troublesome situation with a parent.

An ideal situation would be one in which the school's administrators, teachers, and counselors were educated about the effects of family alcoholism on children, and the school had developed, with the help of concerned parents, a plan for providing these children of alcoholics with the education and support they need to cope effectively in school and at home.

In summary, the fact that school personnel are recognizing the need to help children of alcoholics is encouraging. School personnel should take into consideration the needs of the children, the extent of cooperation of the parents, the risks involved if parental consent can't be obtained, and the resources of time and staff available when deciding the kind and extent of help that will be offered to these children.

An important caution

Whatever the group setting a child should always be cautioned not to confront a parent about drinking unless he or she does so under the guidance and protection of a knowledgeable adult who can provide protection and support to the child. It is important to emphasize to the children that *it is not safe for a child to talk with an alcoholic parent about the drinking if the child is alone and/or if the parent has been drinking.* Since a child is not alway the best judge of whether or not a parent has been drinking, or whether or not he or she is in danger of being hurt, this point should be re-emphasized periodically.

Suggestions for setting up groups

Previous sections have set forth the workbook's objectives and possible uses in a variety of settings. This section includes practical suggestions for setting up a group—finding an appropriate room; choosing a group leader; determining age levels; size of the group; number and length of sessions; explaining the group to parents; obtaining parental permission; reporting child abuse and neglect; working with children with special learning needs.

The next chapter will include a list of objectives for each session and ideas for using each chapter with the children.

Physical setting

Leaders usually can make do with whatever room is available in a school or agency. Many churches and community centers are cooperative in providing space for groups. A carpeted room with large throw pillows or bean bag chairs provides a quiet and comfortable setting.

Ages of children

As said before, the activities in the workbook are designed for children from seven to early adolescence. As there are differences in children's cognitive, social, and emotional development at these ages, group leaders will need to use their own judgment in setting age ranges and in adapting materials and activities to fit their particular group. Children in this age group will have varied abilities in reading too. For this reason, the workbook should be read aloud by the leader with the children. Or some children may volunteer to read aloud.

Size of group

Ultimately the decision of group size will depend on children's ages, the number of leaders, and individual circumstances. Groups of three to eight children have been found to be a comfortable size for this age group.

Number and length of sessions

Although the workbook activities can be adapted to fit whatever time frames are established, reading the book and doing the activities usually require about six to nine sessions of sixty to ninety minutes in length. If sessions are run concurrently with an adult program, you may not have a choice about the length of the group sessions. But if you vary activities and have occasional breaks, the length of the session need not be a major problem. Some groups have been run successfully with one hour sessions. Others have been scheduled for two-hour sessions with planned refreshment or rest breaks.

Group leaders

The group leader who guides these children through The Children's Book is the single most important influence in helping them. Although The Children's Book and suggested activities can be a catalyst for children to begin to discuss their problems, it is the leader who will have the greatest effect on what and how the children learn. An effective group leader should:

- create a relaxing environment which encourages the children to trust, to talk, to listen, and to feel;

- have the abilities to listen well, and to express genuinely both positive and negative feelings;

- empathize with the children's feelings without pitying them;

- set clear and consistent limits;

- establish trust;

- convey acceptance of the children;

- observe and offer feedback on the children's behavior and interactions in the group;

- respect the uniqueness and individuality of each child;

- be flexible and have a good sense of humor and playfulness.

When working with children of this age, the leader should understand that this role is primarily that of a facilitator who encourages children to see family problems in a new light and who models more effective ways of expressing feelings and coping with problems. The group leader should encourage the children to learn new problem-solving and decision-making skills, as well as offering them reinforcement and support for healthy ways in which they are already handling their problems.

The group leader's responsibility is to foster independence rather than dependence. Because many children of alcoholics are not receiving adequate parenting, it is tempting for a group leader to slip into a parental role and attempt to take over some of these responsibilities. This however can be detrimental to the child because it sets up unrealistic expectations that the group leader usually cannot sustain over time. A good rule is: Don't promise more than you can deliver. Many of these children have been disappointed by broken promises often enough that their ability to trust is impaired. The group leader should be open, honest, and realistic about what he or she can and cannot give.

It is especially important that adults who are considering becoming group leaders come to terms with their own childhood conflicts and unresolved emotional issues. The helping professions seem to have a disproportionately large number of adults who grew up in families where alcoholism, neglect, or abuse influenced their own development. These helpers' own childhoods can help them empathize and understand the children's problems, but first they must have acknowledged and accepted their own experiences and learned how to express feelings, communicate, cope with problems, and relate in healthy ways.

Many survivors of alcoholic or abusive families have never come to terms with their own pain, anger, and unmet needs. Some of these adults move into helping positions as an unconscious way of working out their own unresolved problems. Others may want to help these children because they are unconsciously operating on the assumption that "if I take care of others, someone will take care of me." Some simply may be acting out in adulthood the "caretaking" roles they adopted as children—to try to take away the pain of others without giving adequate attention to their own pain and needs.

Potential group leaders are reminded that you can seldom give to another what you don't have for yourself. To give these children hope and skills for coping with their problems, you too must have hope and skills. Adult children of alcoholics who wish to be group leaders should read Claudia Black's *It Will Never Happen to Me!*. Written for adults who have grown up in alcoholic families, it contains information and exercises to help them come to terms with childhood experiences and to recognize how these experiences affect current relationships. These adults may need to seek help from professional counselors who understand alcoholism's effects on family systems and development. Participating in an Al-Anon group and working the Twelve Steps (as adapted for families of alcoholics from the Twelve Steps of Alcoholics Anonymous) can be helpful. Facing up to the effects of a childhood in an alcoholic family seems to involve "unlearning" those three unspoken rules (don't talk, don't trust, don't feel) identified by Claudia Black. This "coming to terms" also involves recognizing one's own sadness, grieving for a childhood that wasn't all one hoped for or deserved, forgiving one's parents, and letting go of anger and resentment for any injustices or abuse or neglect.

Group leaders must be able to do what they want the children to do: recognize their feelings, ask for help, and trust that others can be counted on to respond to their feelings and needs.

The group leader is encouraged to find a coleader or assistant leader. This person can be valuable in helping children with activities and in providing support, feedback, and assistance with behavior problems. If a colleague is not available, a capable volunteer can be recruited from a local college or from Alateen or Al-Anon. A leader should be sure to review the workbook and its goals with the assistant leader prior to working together.

Explaining groups to parents

Since interaction with parents is important, whenever possible leaders should first meet individually with parents to explain the program. An initial meeting for all parents can then follow with a "touch-base" kind of supportive, informative relationship between leader and parents continuing for the length of the program.

In most cases, leaders will find it wise, if not necessary, to obtain parental permission for children of this age to participate in a support group. Parents are sometimes hesitant to give permission, for even when the alcoholism/chemical dependency has been acknowledged, many parents deny, minimize, or sincerely do not recognize the effects it has had on their children. Whether parents are alcoholic or co-alcoholic, admitting that alcoholism has affected their children opens a Pandora's box of guilt and shame. Usually this parental denial is easy to maintain because the majority of children of alcoholics are not acting out their frustrations or having behavior problems. They are not talking to their parents about the drinking, the behaviors surrounding it, and their own feelings and fears and needs.

Parents sometimes fear that participation in a group will lead children to realize how bad things are at home. But parents often don't realize that their children already know much more about what is happening in the family than they give them credit for knowing.

To help parents feel more comfortable about permitting their children's participation in the group, present the goals of the children's groups in a positive way, emphasizing—both at individual meetings with parents and at the parents' first group meeting—that the primary purposes are to help children feel better about themselves and their families and to understand more about alcoholism.

A group meeting will help parents see that theirs is not the only family coping with alcoholism. This is best done in a small group setting with comfortable chairs, coffee, and a chance for give-and-take conversation.

During this initial meeting with parents, group leaders should present the objectives of the group and give parents the opportunity to look through The Children's Book and activities. As a preliminary to explaining the workbook, group leaders may wish to read aloud the letter to parents at the beginning of The Children's Book. Encourage parents to ask questions or state any concerns they may have now or at any time during the course of the group sessions.

Often the tone of this meeting is more important than what is actually said. Parents are more agreeable to letting their children take part if they see the leaders as nonjudgmental, helpful, and caring about parents as well as their children, *not* as parent substitutes usurping parental roles or responsibilities. (As an indication of these limits, group leaders should be responsible for children only while they are in group, not while they are in a waiting room or hallway with their parents.)

Let parents know that their children may be uncomfortable at times during the groups, as the activities and information, as well as feelings expressed by other children, may bring to the surface uncomfortable feelings and memories that the children have tried to repress. Reassure both parents and children that children will not be pushed to talk or to participate in activities if they don't feel like talking or taking part, that it is okay to pass their turns in group. Ask parents to notify group leaders if a child seems upset or does not want to continue in the group sessions.

Leaders should remind parents that, just as it's difficult for parents to acknowledge the alcoholism, it is hard for their children too. Suggest to parents that they let their children know that it's all right to talk about their problems in the group.

Parents have valuable information about their children. Group leaders may want to design a questionnaire for parents to provide background information that can help the leaders work more effectively with the children. Some questions you may want to include:

- Who is alcoholic or chemically dependent in the family?

- Is this person actively using alcohol or other drugs at this time?

- Is he or she in a recovery program?

- Are the parents married? Separated? Divorced?

- With whom does the child live? (List all family members and the ages of other siblings.)

- How old? In what grade is your child?

- Has he or she been experiencing any behavior or academic problems in school?

- Is it all right to contact the school to share information on the child's needs and progress? (If parent says yes, release of information forms should be signed.)

- Is the school aware of the alcohol problem in the family?

- Is the child participating in counseling at school?

- Does your child have any health problems, such as allergies?

- What do you hope your child will gain from the group?

- Is it all right to call you at work? At home?

Group leaders should review with parents the "Keeping Confidences" chapter of The Children's Book, (see "Confidentiality" section in the next chapter). If this is not explained, some parents may be upset when they ask their children what happened in group that day and they get the reply, "I can't tell you." Both parents and children should be told that it is okay to discuss the group activities in a general way ("we heard a story and talked about feelings") but that it's not all right to discuss other people's family problems. Parents should be encouraged to respect their children's privacy too and not press them to tell what they talked about in group. Also, this section lets parents know that leaders are legally responsible for reporting suspected abuse and neglect.

As the program continues, parents need to know that as their children learn about alcoholism the children not only may confront problems surrounding the drinking differently, but they may be more vocal about their feelings and perceptions. If one parent is still an active alcoholic, the non-drinking parent should emphasize to the child (as the group leader has done) that it is not safe for the child to talk to the parent about the drinking unless the non-drinking parent is present and the alcoholic has not been drinking.

Group leaders should explain that the purpose of "homework" assignments (see next chapter), if these are to be utilized in the group, is to help children realize that they have power over their own lives; that they can help improve relationships within their families and can feel better. At the end of each children's group, leaders should review briefly the homework assignment with parents to make sure it is feasible and acceptable.

Group leaders should encourage parents to find help for themselves through Al-Anon, AA, and concerned persons groups, if they are not already doing so. Parents also should be given information on community resources for parent education classes, such as Parent Effectiveness Training (PET) or Systematic Training for Effective Parenting (STEP), and on parent support groups, such as Parents without Partners and Parents Anonymous. Also share with parents information about agencies and resources for children, like Alateen, Alatot, Al-Anon, Big Brothers or Big Sisters.

Most important of all, as we said before, group leaders should reassure the adults that they are being responsible parents in allowing their children this opportunity.

Using The Children's Book
with an individual child

Developing children's groups takes time and energy, commodities already stretched to the limit for many busy teachers and counselors. Given these limitations, what can you do to help these children? If you don't have the time or other resources necessary to run a group for these children, or if only one or two children have been identified, you can adapt The Children's Book for individual use. Read the book with the child and do the activities together. If you don't have time to complete the entire book, you may want to emphasize the following:

From Chapter 1:

- Alcoholism is a disease.

- It is not your fault. You cannot make someone alcoholic.

- It is not the alcoholic's fault either. He or she didn't choose to have the disease.

- Alcoholics can recover from the disease, if they get help from AA or another treatment program.

- You cannot stop alcoholics from drinking, nor can you force them to get help.

From the Introduction and Chapter 6:

- You are not alone. Lots of other kids live in families where alcoholism is a problem.

From Chapters 3, 4, and 5:

- You deserve to be helped and you can get help for yourself.

- There are people who will understand.

- You can feel better about yourself.

- Life can be better for you whether or not your parent stops drinking.

Reporting child abuse and neglect

Newspapers and television bring us all too frequent accounts of maltreatment and violence within families. In fact, the family has been described as the most violent social group, and the home the most violent setting, in our society (Straus, Gelles, and Steinmetz, 1980). Family violence can be defined as behavior which harms or has the intent of harming another family member (or other family members) physically or emotionally. Neglect, closely related to family violence, is the withholding of or the failure to provide what is necessary for normal growth and development. Neglect can scar a child as severely as physical abuse.

Reports of neglect and abuse have skyrocketed since states have provided child-abuse hotlines, safe houses, counseling, and other resources for abused children. Communities seem to be awakening to these problems, but it is likely that only a very small percentage come to the attention of those who can help.

All states now have child abuse and neglect legislation. Before beginning the group program, leaders should call the local child protective agency or division of family services to ask for a copy of their state's child abuse statute. States vary slightly in their child abuse legislation, but generally the laws provide for a hotline and for immunity from prosecution for persons who call in and report suspected neglect or abuse. Child protection agencies do not expect callers to have witnessed firsthand actual incidents. The expectation is that those concerned over possible abuse or neglect situations will pass on their concern to the agency charged with the responsibility of investigating. Teachers, physicians, counselors, and other helping persons are mandated by law to report possible abuse or neglect. Group leaders should check with their local child protection agencies to determine their status on mandated reporting.

Bruises, burns, or other marks on a child can be signals of abuse. If a child seems to have difficulty walking or is uncomfortable sitting, it could mean physical or sexual abuse has occurred. Even faced with distressing signs like these and the possibility of a child's having been abused, some people still hesitate to report it. The responsibility for treatment is shared by medical, judicial, and social service professions, but the problems cannot be remedied and treatment systems cannot function if the agency responsible is not informed. In a broader sense, all adults are responsible for the welfare of children they know.

Adults working with children of alcoholics have a special responsibility, since alcoholism in a family can make the household an unsafe place in which to live, especially for children.

Because neglect and abuse can occur in alcoholic families, it is wise for group leaders to work out a procedure and establish a good relationship with child protection services agencies, then, after reporting an instance of suspected abuse, inform the appropriate agency if follow-up and treatment does not take place.

Since treatment of an alcoholic family may be a long-term, up-and-down process, leaders need to report a possible abusive incident even though the family already is in counseling or treatment.

Working with handicapped children

At least ten percent of school-aged children have special learning needs because of a handicapping condition (a physical handicap; hearing, speech, or visual impairment; learning disabilities; mental retardation). Because of the likelihood of your working with a handicapped child in your group, and because alcoholism itself can be the cause of some handicapping conditions as in FAS children, we include the following suggestions on how to help handicapped children benefit from The Children's Book and the group experience.

If the child's handicap is obvious, explain it to the other children since children this age are usually outspoken and curious about obvious differences. In order to avoid embarrassing the handicapped child, ask the child's permission to do this *before* the group begins. You might say, "John, some of the children may be curious about your hearing aids. Is it okay with you if I explain what they are, so that the other children will understand?" Or you could ask the child if he would prefer to explain them himself, with your help. Talking about the handicap provides an opportunity to present the child to the group in a positive way, by emphasizing how the child is like other children.

Offer suggestions to the other children on how best to include the child in the group discussions and activities. You might say, "Of course, we want everyone in the group to be able to participate. When you talk, be sure to let John see your faces so that he can read your lips, but you don't need to talk louder than you usually do."

Physical disabilities may include muscular dystrophy, cerebral palsy, injuries to the spinal cord resulting in paralysis of legs and/or arms, epilepsy, birth defects or injuries resulting in loss of limbs, and others. To help a physically disabled child, ask the parent about the child's specific limitations. Ask if the child will need assistance toileting. If you plan to serve refreshments, ask if there are dietary restrictions. During the group, matter-of-factly explain the child's disability. "Mike lost his arm in an accident, so now he writes with his other hand." Or "Susie is in a wheelchair because she can't walk. When it's time for us to move, we'll push her chair."

Visual impairments range from the inability to see printed pages to blindness. Read the workbook aloud so that children themselves don't need to read in order to follow along. Give a visually impaired child paper and pens or markers of contrasting colors so that he can more easily see what he's writing. For the blind child, record her answers (or enlist the help of another child to do so), then ask the group to share their answers and describe the drawings orally.

Hearing impairments can mean anything from a mild hearing loss for certain tones and voices to total deafness. Since language acquisition has been hard for them, many hearing impaired and deaf children also have reading and speech problems. Pantomime and drawings can help them express their ideas and feelings. Most deaf children lipread, but since only forty percent of English speech is visible this way, lip-reading involves much guesswork and heavy concentration. Check to be sure the child is understanding what is being said by noting facial expressions and by asking pertinent questions occasionally. To lip-read effectively the child must see the speaker's face without a play of shadows or glare from lights. (Overhead lighting usually is best.) If the child is deaf and uses sign language, an interpreter should attend the groups with the child. Explain to the group that the interpreter will sign their words to the child, and the child's signs will be voiced by the interpreter. Instruct children to talk directly to the deaf child rather than to the interpreter. The interpreter should sit across from the child so that the child can see easily.

Since children with *speech problems* may be reluctant to join in group activities, the leader can encourage their participation by waiting patiently while the child tries to talk. Or the group leader can encourage expression by providing ways to do an activity—writing, drawing, or charades—as alternatives for speaking. Giving these options to all the children adds variety and interest, as well as allowing the speech-handicapped child to pick the most comfortable option without feeling different from the others.

Mentally retarded children have not only below average intellectual abilities but also deficits in adaptive social behaviors. Since the degree of mental retardation varies from child to child, the group leader and parents should decide if the group is appropriate for the child, based on the child's ability to understand the information and activities. Sometimes a slightly older mentally retarded child might be included in this age group if the group seems suited to the child's needs. So that the child's academic problems do not interfere with participation, the group leader should read the activities aloud, and offer alternatives to writing answers (role-playing, charades, drawing pictures, or having the leader write answers at the child's direction). Also, the mentally retarded child may need specific feedback on appropriate behavior and social skills.

A child with *a specific learning disability* may have average or above intelligence but exhibits a disorder in one or more of the basic processes involved in understanding or using spoken or written language. These may be exhibited in disorders of listening, thinking, talking, reading, writing, spelling, or arithmetic. They include conditions referred to as perceptual handicaps—brain injury, minimal brain dysfunction, dyslexia, developmental aphasia, etc. Characteristics of the learning disabled child may include hyperactivity, perceptual-motor impairments, emotional lability, general coordination deficits, disorders of attention, impulsivity, as well as disorders of memory or of language, and specific learning problems in certain academic areas.

Some learning-disabled children have perceptual problems that not only make reading hard for them, but also keep them from readily perceiving differences in facial expressions or tones of voice or touches. For instance, a learning-disabled child who cannot perceive subtle differences in facial expressions may confuse a frown and a smile. A child who cannot hear the differences in tones of voices may not understand the emotional message that is being sent. A child who confuses kinds of touch may hug someone too forcefully or feel irritated by a friendly pat on the back. The child who is hyperactive may have difficulty sitting quietly and listening.

Learning-disabled children need activities presented in a variety of ways: visually, auditorially, and with demonstration and role playing. Read the workbook with the children and demonstrate how to do the activities. Also, the group leader can provide alternatives to writing, drawing, and speaking. Some examples would be "sculpturing" family roles by asking other group members to be "statues" of their family, or using pantomime to express their feelings. For children who get overexcited easily, take a relaxation break by having the children lean back in their chairs, take deep breaths, and count slowly for a short time.

And remember, in summary:

1. The setting in which you work will influence the way in which you use the materials.

2. Both children and parents will have questions initially and these should be answered fully and honestly.

3. The child should not be expected to be the agent for family change.

4. Since school personnel have direct access to children and responsibility for their education and support, schools will need to consider the parent consent issue as it applies to them.

5. Adults who are considering becoming group leaders must have come to terms with their own childhood conflicts and unresolved emotional issues. Potential leaders owe it to themselves and to the children to first work out their own difficulties.

6. Leaders should, whenever possible, encourage parents' involvement and support by meeting with them individually to explain the program; meeting with them informally as a group at the start of the program; continuing to keep them informed individually about homework and their children's general reaction to the group.

7. Parents should realize that children who are participating in the groups may now be more open with their questions and perceptions at home.

8. The confidentiality of the group needs to be understood by parents.

9. The "homework" can provide a positive interaction between parent and child—the opportunity to get and give praise.

10. Parents need to be reassured that they are being good parents in offering this opportunity to their children.

11. Leaders need to know the child-abuse legislation in their own state and to develop a relationship with local child protective services.

12. Handicapped children and those with specific learning disabilities can be part of the group but will need special attention.

Chapter Five
Using The Children's Book

The Children's Book and its suggested activities are designed as a framework for beginning to develop a children's group.

Of course, the material may be modified to meet the needs of the particular children with whom you work. These needs will vary depending upon the children's ages, whether or not parents are recovering—if not, how far a parent's disease has progressed and the setting (school, treatment center, or other agency). If you wish to add more information to the program, references on pages 123-125 and the Suggested Reading on page 126 in The Children's Book may be helpful.

Try to avoid using the children's workbook as a literal "recipe book," expecting that if kids understand all the information and fill in all the blanks, somehow their problems will be "fixed." Instead use your own personality, creativity, humor, and counseling style. In the end, your humanity, caring, support, and modeling of honest communication will have the greatest effect on what the children learn with you.

As you continue to use The Children's Book, you will develop the style and methods that are most comfortable and useful for you and the children. Being flexible and attentive to children's needs at all times is especially important. You may find that some activities work well with some groups but not as well with others.

If you do not get through all the material allotted for a session, either pick up where you left off at the next session, or go over the summarizing review at the end of the chapter.

Note: As mentioned earlier, this workbook is intended to be read *with* the children, rather than by them independently. The reading level may be too difficult for some children this age, and the material requires guidance to help children understand.

Initial session:

Objectives

1. Children and group leaders will get to know each other and feel more comfortable with each other.

2. Children will agree upon group rules and about keeping confidences.

3. Children will realize they are not alone, that other children live in families with problem drinkers.

4. Children will learn that alcohol is a drug that has certain effects on the mind and the body.

5. Children will learn that alcoholism is a disease.

6. Children will learn that they are not to blame for their parents' alcoholism.

Activity: Name game introduction

Instructions: Think of three things that tell something about yourself and your family. The first person will say his name, then three things about himself. For example: "My name is Paul. I have two brothers and a sister, I like to shoot baskets and I love to swim." Then the next person gives her name, three things about herself, and the first person's name and at least one thing he said about himself. Continue around the group in this fashion with each person picking up and repeating the name and one thing about that person who has just spoken. For example: "My name is Cheryl. I like to swim and give puppet plays, and I have three sisters and a brother. This is Paul. He likes to shoot baskets."

After the name game, read the Introduction to the workbook. Review the rules of the group. Add any rules that the group decides—or that you know—are needed.

Confidentiality

Explain "confidentiality" to the children. (Briefly review confidentiality and other group rules at the beginning of each session.) You may wish to introduce the concept of confidentiality by reading the "Keeping Confidences" section in The Children's Book. Then add a statement like this:

> "One of the purposes of this group is for us to learn to share our feelings with other people so that we can help each other. In order for us to be able to respect and trust each other, it is important for us to agree not to tell other people outside our group what someone shares with this group. This means we will not say to other people things like 'Do you know what Johnny's mother and father did?' or 'Guess what Susan said?' The things we say in group are private. It's okay to tell parents what *you* said or did in the group but it's not okay to tell what other kids shared. What they share is their *own*, and belongs to them, they are the only ones who should share their own confidences.

I will keep this trust too, but it is also my responsibility to help see that you are safe and protected. If you tell me about abuse (being hurt or seriously neglected), I am required to report this to people at the agency in charge of protecting children so that they can see that you are safe. Except for reporting incidents of abuse, I will not tell other people outside this group what you say unless I have your permission first."

If you are associated with an agency or treatment center that works with entire families, you may also want to explain to the children that you may share relevant information with other agency counselors in order to help the family. You could say: "Sometimes, when something important to you or your family is discussed, I may let the counselor working with your family know."

Chapter 1: Drinking and Drugs

Read this chapter aloud to the children. Have them do the activities as you go.

Page 1. Drugs that change a person's moods are: marijuana, alcohol, heroin, Librium, and Valium. Answers to "Can You Guess?": 1. alcohol, 2. marijuana, 3. Librium and Valium.

Page 4. Drinking parent quiz: Since this quiz is not a diagnostic questionnaire, it does not matter how many yes or no answers the child marks. Use the quiz to stimulate discussion about how children in alcoholic families often feel. Don't label a child's parent as alcoholic if that person has not yet been identified openly as such. Some children still may not have accepted the existence of a parent's drinking problem. Allow children to come to this acceptance. The object of this quiz is for children to hear the information and have the opportunity to consider whether or not it applies in their own lives. Remember that the "don't talk, don't trust, don't feel" rules are strong, and children differ in their readiness to talk about the problem. The group leader needs to realize that children don't need to speak openly about their home situation in order to be helped.

Page 6. Talk with the children about their feelings of blame for the drinking. Whom are they blaming? Are they blaming themselves? If they feel they are to blame, find out what they saw or did that made them think the drinking was their fault.

Homework assignment

The purpose of this assignment is to help children realize they have some control over how they feel and what they do:

Write down a list of ten things you enjoy doing that help you feel good about yourself.

Do at least one of these things for fifteen minutes each day. Keep a list of what you did.

(The group leader and child should review the list with the parent so that the parent understands the assignment, and agrees that all items listed are all right for the child to do.)

Chapter 2: Feelings

Objectives

1. Help children learn that everyone has both comfortable and uncomfortable feelings.

2. Help children recognize, accept, and share their feelings.

3. Help children recognize how they handle their feelings.

4. Help children identify constructive ways to handle feelings.

5. Help children identify people in their lives to share their feelings with.

6. Help children recognize and understand the defenses they use.

7. Help children understand what blackouts are and who may have them.

Page 10. The children may enjoy acting out the story about Fuzzy as it is read to them. Have them choose parts: Fuzzy, his friends (any number), Butch, Mom, Dad, and RAS. Use large squares of paper with feeling words written on them. Have the children tape them onto the "cocoon" as the story progresses. They can tear them off as Fuzzy learns to share his feelings. Discuss what feelings the children decided were comfortable. (Their ideas probably will vary.) Discuss how some people are more comfortable than others with expressing certain feelings. Be nonjudgmental and accepting of children's answers.

Homework assignment

Tell children, "Share with your parent for ten minutes each day what you did that day. Share one feeling you felt that day. Then ask your parent to share his or her day and one feeling. Remember when sharing feelings: Don't judge other people's feelings. They are *their* feelings, and they have a right to them. Don't tell people how they should or should not feel. Feelings are not good or bad, right or wrong. They just *are*. We don't control our feelings, we *do* control our actions."

Chapter 3: Families

Objectives

1. Help children recognize how they feel about their families.

2. Help children realize they are not alone, that other children also may share these feelings about their families.

3. Help children understand that families and family members are alike in some ways, different in others. Living in a family feels different for each member, but many feelings may be shared.

4. Help children improve their relationships with brothers and sisters.

5. Give children practice in expressing feelings and offering feedback.

Because there is a lot of material in this chapter, you may want to break it into two sessions, one concentrating on family, parents, and rules, and the other on brothers and sisters.

Page 23. Drawing the family: The counselor should try not to read too much into the drawings but to note the following:

1. Where is the child in relation to other family members? Here you can ask the child which persons he or she feels closest to.

2. Who is in the center of the family picture?

3. Is a family member left out of the picture?

4. What are the expressions on the faces of the people in the family?

5. What other items are in the picture (beer bottles, for instance).

As you look at the drawings, remember that sometimes children draw pictures of how they *want* the family to be, rather than how the family seems to them now.

Ask the children to talk about their pictures so that you can check out your interpretations. One way to do this is by saying "Tell me about your picture. What are the people feeling?"

Page 24. Family rules: Discuss the rules the children have written. Which ones are similar? Which ones are different from one family to the next? Summarize what the children have in common.

Page 25. Unspoken rules: Many of the children may mention the unspoken rule of not talking about the drinking. Discuss their confusing feelings toward their families. If children are hesitant to talk about their own situations, discuss Shauna's confusion. Why do you think Shauna felt as if things were "kind of crazy?"

Family feelings

Discuss confusing feelings of loving and hating the same person. Restate that it is natural to feel both ways when someone's behavior changes from one extreme to another. Do not be surprised if some of the children find their alcoholic parent more tolerable when drunk than sober. You can use that opportunity to reinforce the idea that people who are not comfortable with their feelings—even with affectionate, nice feelings—may drink to feel more comfortable.

Page 25. Talk about what the children do with their confusing feelings. Then discuss the advantages/disadvantages of each alternative. Example: Holding feelings inside may cause headaches, stomachaches, and loneliness.

Talking to someone about your feelings can help you feel less alone and that person might be able to comfort you.

Brothers and sisters

Page 26. Children bring their brothers and sisters to this group session. Brothers and sisters under four years of age may be hard to incorporate into the group, but no upper limit in age is necessary. Some group members have ranged from four to twenty-eight years of age, but all have a right to be considered equal, since they are there as brothers or sisters.

If siblings are coming to the group for the first time, you may want to review briefly the goals of the group and do a "warm-up" activity such as the name game from Session 1.

Let siblings know you are glad they came. Tell them that in alcoholic families, brothers and sisters sometimes seem to feel isolated from each other and fight a lot. That is sad, because they could really make things less lonely and more comfortable for each other. Tell them the purpose of the next few activities is to help them understand each other better.

Make extra copies of each workbook activity in this section for siblings so that each child has individual worksheets. Older brothers and sisters can help younger ones with writing. Re-emphasize that this is not school; if they have trouble spelling, they can just *pretend* they can spell.

Have brothers and sisters share their answers. Be sure to emphasize that there are no right or wrong answers, and that people feel things in different ways even in the same family.

Page 29. Happy/mad/sad/hurt activity: You may want to encourage the children to do this activity orally, since talking may be less complicated than writing it down. Take one sibling at a time. "How do the rest of you know when John is mad? What does he look like? Say? Do?"

Sometimes siblings will say they cannot tell when brother John is hurt or sad or mad. Ask John if he knew this. Point out that many times people expect others to know how they feel, even though they don't show their feelings. When we do not share our feelings, it is not reasonable to expect that others will respond or comfort us. Ask John what he would like his brothers and sisters to do when he is mad or hurt or sad?

Page 31. Even if you are pressed for time, be sure to include this activity about what brothers and sisters *like* about each other. Frequently siblings have only discussed what they do *not* like (and usually it has been discussed very loudly!) The children may be embarrassed to say what they like about each other. You can use this opportunity to discuss why is it that it is easier to tell someone that he or she is a "dirty, rotten, no good jerk" than it is to say what is liked or appreciated about the person. Ask each child which kind of comment he or she would rather hear about himself/herself.

Homework assignment

Have the children write down two nice things they could do for mom or dad or brothers or sisters this week. Review them with parents to be sure they are acceptable and "do-able."

Chapter 4: Coping with Problems

Objectives

1. Children will be given the opportunity to discuss problems in their families.

2. Children will understand some effective ways of coping with these problems.

This session is a discussion session. You can read together the problems and discuss choices of how to handle them. Be sure to give the children plenty of time to relate the sample situations to their own problems and to discuss their own feelings and ways of coping. To involve the children actively, translate some of the problems into role plays. Be sure to let each child write a problem of his/her own, then get suggestions from the group about how to handle it.

Homework assignment:

Have each child select one of his or her own problems and follow through on the group's suggestion. Ask each one to report the following week on what happened.

Chapter 5: Changes

Objectives

1. Help children realize they cannot control or change another person. This includes a parent with a drinking problem.

2. Help children realize that they *do* have control over themselves. They have power to change their own lives.

3. Help children differentiate between things they can change and things they cannot.

4. Help children realize that there are people who care about them and are willing to help them. Help children identify these people.

5. Help children realize that recovery from alcoholism takes time. The situation in an

alcoholic family will not improve right away.

Most of the activities in this chapter are self-explanatory. While doing them with the children, reinforce the objectives stated above.

Homework assignment

Have the children keep a daily diary of what they tried to change, the persons they asked to help them (if they did), and how things turned out.

Chapter 6: Choices

Objectives

1. Help children realize that, although they cannot always choose what happens to them, they can choose how they react.

2. Help children improve their decision-making skills.

3. Help children realize that they do not have to be limited by the past. They can learn new ways to think and act.

4. Help children realize their strengths and skills.

5. Introduce children to whatever other support or aftercare groups including Ala-tot and Ala-teen are available in the community.

Page 53. You may ask the children to act out the story about Matt and Peter.

Page 57. Tom's decision: Try to avoid stating your personal views initially. Let the children go through the thought process.

Some of your group members already may be on the way to addiction. The number of elementary-aged children who are alcoholic/chemically dependent is on the rise. Be open to their concerns and questions. Anne Snyder's book for children, *Kids and Drinking,* has a useful self-quiz for children to help them see if they are in trouble with alcohol. While such self-quizzes have obvious drawbacks, they can be a starting point for helping the addicted person.

Evaluation

You may want to use the evaluation sheet on page 67 to obtain information from participants about how to improve the groups. Use page 69 to send suggestions to the authors. They would welcome ideas from children and adults about *The Elephant in the Living Room* books. The form can be cut out and mailed to the publisher.

The end or the beginning?

Children often are saddened by the ending of the group program. To help ease the "separation anxiety," plan a pizza party, movie, or some other reunion event at a date several weeks later. Children of appropriate ages for Alateen (or Alatot, if your community has one) can make an agreement to attend their first meeting together. Of course, you may choose to keep the group together, to extend the length of the program using selected exercises from The Children's Book occasionally or from resources listed in Suggested Reading.

The last meeting of the group can also be an occasion to fill in the certificates of completion (at the back page of the workbook). A gold paper sticker and a bit of ribbon affixed to the "diploma" will contribute a sense of accomplishment and ceremony.

About the authors

Marion H. Typpo is Assistant Professor of Human Development and Family Studies at the University of Missouri in Columbia, where she teaches courses in adolescence and early adulthood, family development, adulthood and aging, and violence in the family. She holds a Ph.D. in Child and Family Development from the University of Missouri, an M.A. in Counseling and Psychology from the University of Minnesota in Minneapolis, and a B.A. in Psychology and Sociology from the University of Minnesota in Duluth.

She is a Board Member of McCambridge Center, a shelter for women who are victims of alcoholism and drug abuse. She is active in campus issues of alcoholism and abuse, serving on an advisory committee to work with students at the University of Missouri. She was asked to lead a workshop in Finland on women's issues and the impact of alcoholism in the family, focusing on women as caretakers. As a result of her involvement in that workshop, *An Elephant in the Living Room* is being used in a program near the Arctic Circle.

Her professional memberships include the American Psychological Association, National Council for Family Relations, American Association for Counseling and Development, and the Missouri Prevention Network.

Jill Hastings has earned her Ph.D. in Human Development and Family Studies from the University of Missouri, Columbia, where she also received her B.S. in Education—in Behavioral Sciences and Rehabilitation Services and her M.S. in Child and Family Development.

Her experience has included teaching, counseling, and curriculum development for the public school system in Columbia, and working with handicapped and disadvantaged adolescents and young adults in rehabilitation programs.

Currently, she is working as a child and family therapist at Youth and Shelter Services in Ames, Iowa. She also works as a counselor in the schools in Ames and coordinates and teaches drug prevention and education programs in the schools there.

Jill Hastings is a Clinical Member of the American Association of Marriage and Family Therapy. She is also a member of the American Association for Counseling and Development, American School Counselors Association, and the International Association of Marriage and Family Counseling.

References

Aldoory, S. (1979). Research into family factors in alcoholism. *Alcohol Health and Research World, 3(4)*, 2-6.

Bane, M.J. (1976). Here to Stay. New York: Basic Books.

Baraga, D.J. (1977). Self-concept in children of alcoholics. (Doctoral dissertation, University of North Dakota). *Dissertation Abstracts International, 39* (1-B), 368 B. (Order No. 7810312).

Bernard, J. (1975). *Women, Wives, Mothers*. Chicago: Aldine.

Black, C. (1979). Children of Alcoholics. *Alcohol Health and Research World, 4(1)*, 23-27.

Black, C. (1981). Innocent bystanders at risk: the children of alcoholics. *Alcoholism, 1*(3), 22-26.

Black, C. (1982). *It Will Never Happen To Me!* Denver: M.A.C.

Deutsch, C. *Broken Bottles, Broken Dreams: Understanding and Helping the Children of Alcoholics*. New York: Teachers College Press.

Elkind, D. (1982). *The Hurried Child*. Addison-Wesley.

Flavell, J.H. (1977). *Cognitive Development*. Englewood Cliffs, N.J.: Prentice-Hall.

Goffman, E. (1959) *The Presentation of Self in Everyday Life.* Garden City, N.Y.: Doubleday.

Hughes, J.M. (1977). Adolescent children of alcoholic parents and the relationship of Alateen on these children. *Journal of Consulting and Clinical Psychology, 45,* 946-947.

Koch, H.L. (1955). Some personality correlates of sex, sibling position and spacing among five- and six-year-old children. *Genetic Psychological Monographs, 52,* 3-50.

Kohlberg, L. (1976). Moral stages and moralization: Cognitive-developmental approach. In T. Lickona (Ed.), *Moral Development and Behavior: Theory, Research and Social Issues.* New York: Holt, Rinehart and Winston, (1972).

Korcok, M. (1981). Children of alcoholics comprise a big share of society's future. *Focus on Alcohol and Drug Issues, 4*(5), 2-3.

McCabe, J. (1977). Children in need: consent issues in treatment. *Alcohol Health and Research World, 2,* 2-12.

Miller, D.M. & Jang, M. (1977) Children of alcoholics: a 20-year longitudinal study. *Social Work and Research Abstracts, 13*(4), 23-29.

Richards, T. (1979). Working with children of an alcoholic mother. *Alcohol Health and Research World, 3*(3), 22-25.

Robe, L. (1982). *Just So It's Healthy.* Minneapolis: Comp-Care Publishers.

Schneiderman, I. (1975). Family thinking in prevention of alcoholism. *Preventive Medicine, 4,* 296-308.

Seidler, G. (1981) 10 million new alcoholics coming down the road. *Focus on Alcohol and Drug Issues, 4*(5), 9-10.

Snyder, A. (1977). *Kids and Drinking.* Minneapolis: Comp-Care Publishers.

Straus, M.A., Gelles, R.J., and Steinmetz, S.K. (1980). *Behind Closed Doors: Violence in the American Family.* New York: Doubleday.

Waller, W. & Hill, R. (1951) The Family: A Dynamic Interpretation, New York: Holt.

Wegscheider, Don (1979). *If Only My Family Understood Me...* Minneapolis: CompCare Publishers.

Wegscheider, Sharon. (1979). Children of alcoholics caught in a family trap. *Focus on Alcohol and Drug Issues, 2,* 8.

Wilson, C. & Orford, J. (1978). Children of alcoholics: a report of a preliminary study and comments on the literature. *Journal of Studies on Alcohol, 39*(1), 121-142.

Woodside, Migs. (1982). Children of alcoholics. A report to Hugh L. Carey, Governor of the State of New York. New York State Division of Alcoholism and Alcohol Abuse.

Additional Resources

Books and Bibliographies for Group Leaders

Ackerman, R. (1978). *Children of Alcoholics: A Guidebook for Educators, Therapists, and Parents.* Holmes Beach, Florida: Learning Publications, Inc.

Cork, R.M. (1969). *The Forgotten Children.* Markham, Ontario, Canada: Paper Jacks, Ltd.

Bormaster, J., & Treat, C. (1982). *Building Interpersonal Relationships through Talking, Listening, Communicating: Group Activities for Students of All Ages.* Austin, Texas: PRO-ED.

New Games Foundation, Fluegelman, A., editor. (1976). *The New Games Book.* Garden City, New York: Doubleday.

Thompson, C., & Ruldolph, L. (1983). *Counseling Children.* Monterey, California: Brooks/Cole Publishing Company.

Woodside, M. "Woodside Report" (bibliographies for children of alcoholics). Available from the Division of Alcoholism and Alcohol Abuse, 194 Washington Avenue, New York, New York 12210.

A Growing Concern: How to Provide Services for Children from Alcoholic Families (1983). Alcohol, Drug Abuse, and Mental Health Association (DHHS Publication

No. ADM 83-1257). Washington, D.C.: U. S. Government Printing Office.

Other Publications

COA Review (newsletter about children of alchoholics). P.O. Box 423, Rutherford, New Jersey 07070.

Thomas W. Perrin, Inc., free catalog of materials about children of alcoholics published six times a year. P.O. Box 423, Rutherford, New Jersey 07070.

Films

"Children of Denial," 28 minutes, color. Alcoholism Children Therapy (ACT), P.O. Box 8536, Newport Beach, California 92660.

"Hope for the Children: Early Intervention with Kids from Alcoholic Homes," 30 minutes, color. Health Communications, Inc., 2119-A Hollywood Boulevard, Hollywood, Florida 33020.

"If You Loved Me," 60 minutes, color; and "Soft is the Heart of a Child," 30 minutes, color. Available for free loan courtesy of Operation Cork, Modern Talking Picture Service, Inc., 5000 Park Street North, St. Petersburg, Florida 33709.

Model Programs for Children of Alcoholics

Children Are People, Inc., 1599 Selby Ave., St. Paul, Minnesota 55104. Besides offering support groups for children of alcoholics ages 5-12, CAP, Inc., offers training workshops throughout the United States to train helping adults to implement, facilitate, and adapt support groups to their own settings.

CASPAR Alcohol Education Program, 226 Highland Avenue, Sommerville, Massachusetts 02143.

Organizations

Al-Anon Family Group Headquarters, P.O. Box 182, Madison Square Station, New York, New York 10010. (Local listings for AA, Al-anon and Alateen can be found in the white or yellow pages of most phone books.)

Alcoholics Anonymous (AA), P.O. Box 459, Grand Central Station, New York, New York 10017.

Big Brothers/Big Sisters of America, 117 S. 17th Street, Suite 1200, Philadelphia, Pennsylvania 19103. (Local affiliates can be found by contacting the national office or the local Family Services of America office.)

Children of Alcoholics Foundation, Inc., 540 Madison Avenue, 23rd floor, New York, New York 10022.

Children of Alcoholics: The New Jersey Task Force, P.O. Box 348, Rutherford, New Jersey 07070.

National Association for Children of Alcoholics, P.O. Box
421961, San Francisco, California 94142.

New York State Coalition for the Children of Alcoholic
Families, P.O. Box 9, Hempstead, New York 11550.

Operation Cork, P.O. Box 9550, San Diego, California
92109. Provides alcohol education materials and films
for families and industry.

Parents Anonymous, 22330 Hawthorne Boulevard, Suite
208, Torrance, California, 90505. PA sponsors self-help
support groups for parents who have or are worried
that they might neglect or abuse their children.